Author: Gaetano Tufolo

LinkedIN Profile: https://www.linkedin.com/in/gaetanotufolo/

Websites:

www.plutusfinancialprotection.com ; www.neptuneyachtsdubai.com

"Get to know yourself. Improve your physical shape. Reach your financial goals"

Summary

Introduction

PART I: Know Yourself. DeTax your Mind.

Chapter 1: The 4 Basic Needs

Chapter 2: The Life Values

Chapter 3: The power of Beliefs

Chapter 4: The puzzle of Personality

PART II: Know your metabolism. DeTax your Body.

Chapter 1: The Efficient Diet

Chapter 2: Macronutrients and Micronutrients

Chapter 3: The essential workout plan

Chapter 4: The essential supplements

PART III: Know your financials. DeTax your Wealth.

Chapter 1: The Quadrants of Cashflow

Chapter 2: Build and DeTax your Personal Network

Chapter 3: The category of assets

Chapter 4: Personal Financials 1.1 and How to Reduce Personal Taxation

Chapter 5: DeTax your time

Chapter 6: How to setup company abroad

Chapter 7: Alternative Investments

Chapter 8: The essentials of running a business

Conclusion

INTRODUCTION

This book came out of the results of many years of experience, simple thoughts and common sense but all put into action.

I always have been a very curious person since I was a child with a habit of reading about new things and then immediately put them into practice because I soon realized that was my learning style.

I did not like listening.
I did not like reading only.
I liked reading and "playing", which is, put into practice what I read.
And that's what I kept doing for the past 12 years.

I started my bachelor's degree studies about 18 years old. I chose business economics as I was always curious to understand people minds behind economic choices and I was always driven by economic news and business books.

At about 19 years old, I start to get bored about just listening to professors and reading books and I soon realized I needed another sparkle to combat my boredom.
I decide to put in practice what I was studying at the university, i.e. I open an investment brokerage account with Fineco, an Italian broker. My first investments were into the stock market, in a period of Crisis (2009)

Now you can understand, at that age I did not have many savings.
hey were just the result of my poor little income that came from small jobs every now and then.
That's when reading a simple quote made everything started.
"Audaces Fortuna Iuvat" latin for "Luck follows the brave".

I had 3,000EUR savings and I decided to invest them all in the stock market and gold.
My first 3 investments were Gold, Apple and Prysmian (an Italian company involved in cables)
Although inexperienced there was a long study about what to choose before investing any EURO.

INTRODUCTION

Gold was a protective investment choice given that we were still in the financial crisis in full.

Keep in mind this was in 2009 so it was an excellent moment to enter the market and I thought of doing so since everything was at the historical minimum.

All 3 investments were profitable.
They were also heavily taxed unfortunately, an analysis that later would condition plenty of my major decisions. The government was taxing my profits, but in case of loss they would not help me in any way. I started to question: Why this is happening after I am bearing 100% of the risk involved?

This was a great kickstart to my investor career.
We will go in details in how I choose my stocks or how I do online trading later in the book.

This was just the beginning of my interest in financial freedom and taxation.

Moving on, eventually I finish my studies, I get my master's degree in business and I start my employee-career in Dubai, UAE. All this while I am growing my stock-market investment account on the side.

Why starting my career in UAE?

Because I did not want to pay any taxes on my income; simple as that.
In UAE there is no personal taxation, so this means that gross salary is equivalent to net salary. There is also no pension obviously, and this means that you have to think yourself about creating your own pension fund.

I also made the calculation that if people in Europe retire at the age of 65 by paying 45% of their personal income in taxes, they could retire before turning 40 if they did not have to pay any tax.

Another important benefit of starting my career as employee in UAE was that this would give me the residence visa.
As UAE resident, I then registered at the AIRE which is the association of Italians residents abroad and I got the freedom to move easily funds between UAE and Italy.. all without any taxation.

Another benefit was that now also my investment in the stock market became totally tax-free. After paying thousands of Euros on my stock market profits this was a great liberation.

INTRODUCTION

Now the profits on my capital gains are not subject anymore to the 27.5% taxation which is applicable in Italy.

It is important to note that being employee was never my goal, but I needed a base to get my first strong financial resources to open eventually my business, so I decided to go through this "path".

My career in Dubai varies from Job to Job.
My first job was in corporate investment banking; since I was already investing in the stock market, I thought it was a great opportunity to learn more.
My position was in accounting and financial controls and I started to get importance in the company.

But my goal was another.

I never wanted to have the employee life with the related 9-5pm working hours, fixed annual holidays and a life commanded by someone else. My need of security was also not primary, as I always valued freedom more over it.

After 2 years of savings I decided to quit and to start on the side my first business venture: Neptune Yachts Rental LLC which is a luxury yacht rental.
Owning luxury goods makes more sense if you can make a business out of it.. that was my thought.

Again, the business is based fully in Dubai, so it does not incur in any taxation.

As you might guess, at the beginning every business venture struggle, so I decided to adapt and to go back on doing another job, this time with the government of one of the seven Emirates.

The job was very close to my expertise as it was in sales and it was related to company formation, things to me familiar as I already had created my own company in Dubai. Through it, I also had the opportunity of meeting investors from everywhere and make some interesting connections.

After another 2 years eventually, I quit also this job, as the yacht business grew up and my paper assets (i.e. investments in the stockmarket) grew up as well.
We are in 2019 and it's time to go full into entrepreneurship.

I open a second company, called Plutus Financial Protection LLC.

INTRODUCTION

The goal of this company is helping people protect their wealth by minimizing taxation and explore the existence of Alternative Investments without high entry-fee barriers.

Plutus helps you obtain tailored solutions regarding the creation and foundation of onshore/offshore/freezone companies, international bank accounts, freelance permits, residence permits and has also investments proposals in private equities (alternative investments).

That's right, that's when I started connecting the two businesses: Yachts Rental and Financial Consulting.

I soon realized that Private Equity could have been considered a very appealing Alternative Investment.

Neptune Yacht Rental LLC was booming and expanding also into water sports.

To inject more capital into the company I decided to give away part of the shares taking in inspiration what companies listed in the stock market do.

Now investors not only benefit of an efficient taxation structure but can also enjoy tax-free income from their alternative investments.

This is me in brief, in the next chapters we will go in details not only in my own story, how I made my decisions, how I chose my investments and what mistakes I made but we will see also different people going through their "path" in another way and perhaps I will change some names to protect their privacy.

Get ready for a journey that will greatly impact your personal finances... obviously if you put into practice the tips and tricks explained.

It is important to keep in mind that this is not just a manual to explain some tips, tricks and investment techniques but wants to be a "journey".
I hope that through reading it you will maybe emphasize with some of the character stories and maybe start to have a different perception of reality that might help you reach your own goals faster.

The objective of the book is not just making money and not pay taxes, but it is to help you create the mental and financial resources to support your dream lifestyle.

INTRODUCTION

Take few seconds and read out loud this sentence: **"to create the resources to support your dream lifestyle".**

And this you can never do it if you are stuck in the highest tax-paying category.

I created a specific term called **"DeTax"**. This means that we will examine ways or remove tax on various aspects of your life, either personal or professional.
DeTax your Mind, DeTax your Body and ultimately... DeTax your wealth.

The zero-tax life management will show you how:

- Not being TAXED from stress, indecisions and debilitating beliefs
- Not being TAXED from extra body weight
- Not being TAXED on your personal income and your corporate income

Without all these types of taxation, you can achieve your dream lifestyle.

The road to wealth is not just about earning more and making more profits... but it is about also:

- Assuming good spending habits
- Protecting your wealth from risks and taxes
- Being open to alternative investments and to increase the sources of your cashflow

The first part of the book will be dedicated into finding yourself and define your dream lifestyle. It is extremely important to align mind and body to your REAL goals.

The second part of the book will be dedicated in how you can achieve the financial support needed to sustain your dream lifestyle.
We will also go through the technicality on how to set-up different types of companies or entities, with the related documents required.

This is an ongoing development book. It is strongly suggested if not mandatory to pause between the chapter. Think. Put in practice what is showed and then continue.

Our brain needs time to assimilate information and even though you might be a reader learner (i.e. a person whose main learning style is reading) to imprint the information in your brain you need to think about it constantly and put into practice when the occasion comes.

The questions you should keep asking yourself are the followings:
"What is my dream lifestyle?" and "What are the resources needed to support it?" "How can I protect my assets to ensure this lifestyle is maintained through time?"

PART I: KNOW YOURSELF. DeTax your Mind.

I decided to open this part of the book with a dedication to yourself and your psychology and your physical well-being while the second part will be the "technical side" and will be called "know your investments".

This is very important, as what might work for me might not work for you or it might work in a different way. Also, before going to do any investment you need to be confident with your personality in order to manage your investment effectively.
Psychology greatly impacts any investment; markets are moved mostly by emotions instead of rational decisions so managing your mind correctly might be your greatest asset.

Statistically, stock market or other investments are governed from the emotions of fear and avidity.

Classic example on how emotion come into play is not selling when your investment is in profit because you are waiting for more profit and not buying a great stock because everything else is going down.

Unfortunately, we are all victim of these two types of emotions and myself I lost a lot of money due to the influence of these 2 emotions. That is why it is important to keep a rational approach to your investments and sometimes if you feel you are influenced by different emotional states of minds, it is better to ask an external consultation about how to behave against a certain investment decision.

Using stop loss/take profit also is a great idea.
Stop loss is an automatic order to sell when a stock goes below a specific price
Take profit is an automatic order to sell when a stock goes above a specific price.

For beginners, I suggest using these two tools in all investments before getting confidence to manage your investments without help of artificial intelligence.

When you are investing, your risk tolerance also comes into play and the way you react to your emotions and the way you plan your actions also determines which category of investments is best suited for you.

For a prospective tactic individual, with a feeling trait, a scale of value with fun scoring high and looking to fulfill his/her basic needs I would never recommend investing in options or derivative instruments for example. Don't worry, soon you will become familiar with the terms and characteristics I just mentioned.

Yes, investment is pure psychology. And your financial consultant should be a good psychologist first before proposing you anything. Investing is not just about choosing the right investment, but also manage your investment effectively. Knowing when to sell, when to buy, or when to increase/decrease own commitment.

Before starting any business, any investment or before taking any major decision you should spend some time into a self-discovery journey. And it might be the best investment of all.

Doing something against own nature is a condemn to a life of unhappiness.

Many authors and many manuals, guides, do not stress enough on this point.

If you think about it, it's pretty much impossible to read success stories of someone that hates his/her profession.
Success stories are about people who align what they love to what they are, and they find the financial ways to do so. We will see many of them in this book as examples.

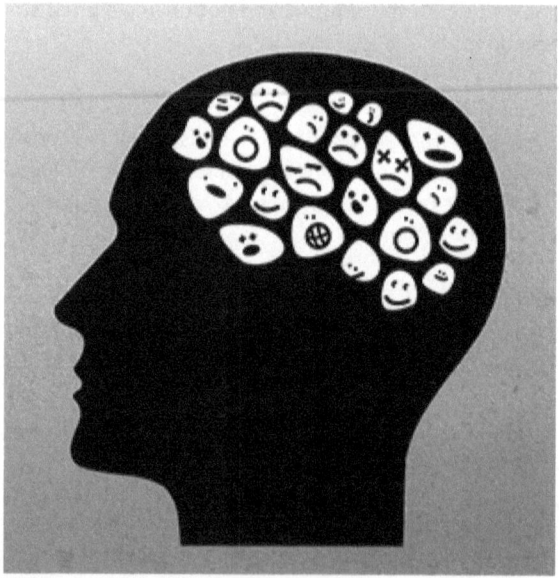

People are different, their values are different, their personality is different. Their physical shape is different, and they produce income from different quadrants.
Therefore, their perception of reality is different.

Chapter 1

The Four basic Needs: To Live, To Learn, To Love, To Leave a Legacy

Believe it or not, all human decisions are around these four needs.

The first basic one is "To Live" which covers all our essential needs.

For some people producing income as Employees, it is considered also the most important need in their perspective, as they value Security over Freedom.

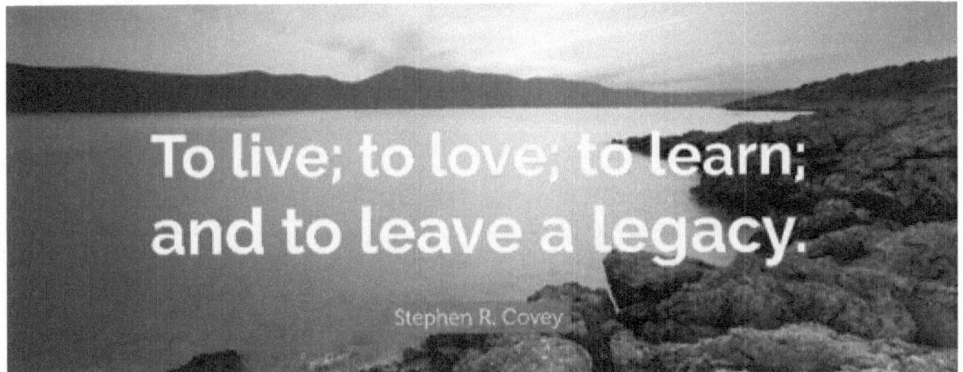

TO LIVE

This need is close to survival as it is about providing the essentials for life which are food, water and shelter.
Therefore, we need to ensure these needs are covered to guarantee our own permanence in this world.

In our age, to obtain them you don't need any more to hunt, to build, to fight like in medieval times but this translates into producing income able to "buy out" food, shelter and water.

School wants to teach us to study, to get a job to pay your student loan and to get a mortgage to buy an house (shelter), work to get enough income to fulfill the basic needs of buying your supplies (food, water) and teach the following generation to do the same.

This might not be the most efficient way to fulfill this need, but it is a way.

Unfortunately, schools do not teach you how to evaluate investments or how to open a business or how to optimize your own personal taxation but teach you only how to become a good employee and how to survive to fulfill your most basic needs.

After all, schools are designed from governments to teach kids how to become good employees and pay a lot of taxes. If you want to be free, you need to learn yourself how you can find different ways to not be manipulated from others.

TO LEARN

Second (not in order of importance as they are all equal) basic need is "to learn".
This responds to the basic human nature of "curiosity".

Look around you, if this need was not strongly implanted in our brain, we would have never been able to create the wheel, the car, the electricity and so on and so forth.

This is what distinguishes us to other creatures in the animal world.
Human mind is curious, wants to understand more, wants to know more.
Another great example would be astronomy.

Imagine even a smart animal like a Dog, although he can learn new tricks if taught so, he will never have the initiative on his own to start to learn how to roll, how to respond to commands or how to jump obstacles.

He will only follow his other 3 needs which are to live (food) to love and to leave a legacy.

Learning is also survival.
Imagine if the man did not learn how to make fire to protect himself against wild animals.

And in economic times, imagine if watch repairers did not learn how to repair also digital watches: they will be pushed out of market.

You reading this book demonstrates the existence of this need, you want to learn something new that might improve the quality of your life.

Updating your skills is a great tool to reduce the risk of your overall portfolio.

TO LOVE

Humans are social animals. Even if you are an introverted person, or a person that prefer solitude or travel solo, this basic need is still in you.
Very few people can handle a life in solitude, that's why is considered one of the most feared punishment the imprisonment in solitude and that's why people in in solitude for too long become crazy.

The need to be loved, as experiments by Bowlby and others have shown, could be considered one of our most basic and fundamental needs. One of the forms that this need takes is contact comfort—the desire to be held and touched. Findings show that babies

who are deprived contact comfort, particularly during the first six months after they are born, grow up to be psychologically damaged.

Given the importance of the need to be loved, it isn't surprising that most of us believe that a significant determinant of our happiness whether we feel loved and cared for. In the surveys that I have conducted, people rate "having healthy relationships" as one of their top goals—on par with the goal of "leading a happy and fulfilling life."

Love covers not only the love you feel for your partner but also the one for your parents, your children, your siblings, your friends and so on and so forth.

Social life is a basic human need. Many of our decisions are made thinking about others, and if you wish to become a business owner you should always consider the repercussions of your decisions on others too.

TO LEAVE A LEGACY

This specific need responds to the creation of family.
Even people who don't have kids might feel a void in them to fulfill this need. That is why not being able to procreate is something that creates much sufferance to certain people.

It is the need for survival as the origin of this idea of wanting to leave a legacy. In the past, people were procreating also for economic reasons: the need of more men to hunt or to work in farms for example. But the reality is also that Humans do not want to be forgotten.

They wanted to be remembered always once their turn to leave is coming. This idea could be a good thought for the one leaving. It was actually a desire to stay forever, although the person can accept the reality that FOREVER is not true for everybody. So, leaving a legacy, so-called, is one form of sentimentalism. It is the person's desire not to be forgotten, and to his mind that is equivalent to existing, even if it was just in the minds of those who were left behind.

It is basic human nature wanting to have a procreation of their own genes also to fulfill a spiritual need to leave something after the ending of own life and perhaps continue their own life through the life of their kids.

This explains why so many sacrifices are done to ensure own kids have a fulfilling life and also why society judges so harshly people who abandon their own kids.

This is a basic explanation of 4 human needs. unconsciously you have always fulfilled them but perhaps ranked in a different way or prioritized in a different way. An university professor might have been focus on his second need mostly for half of his life to obtain his phd, perhaps even sacrificing the first need by sleeping/eating less to spend more times in their research and studies while some people start family very early even before completing their school studies.

What about you? Do you have a financial goal? Do you want to just cover the life basic costs, or you want to live the life of the rich?

How much money do you think you will need to feel completely free from financial stress as your basic needs are covered?

- EXERCISE –

Now, I want you to stop reading.
Stop, because it is mandatory to do some exercise in between the chapters in order to fulfill the final goal of this book that is again, to define your dream lifestyle and to reach the financial support needed to sustain it.

Below some questions, please take the time to write your answers below.

What is the most impellent need you need to focus on for the next 3 years?

Is it to guarantee that you and your family have food and shelter?

Is it to grow professionally climbing a corporate ladder, grow your business or obtain your academic qualification?

Is it to find a partner and to reunite your family? Or to support them through a difficult period?

Is it to start a new family?

Think about it and choose it carefully. I mentioned 3 years, yes.

Why not 1? Statistically people overestimate what they can achieve in a period of one year and underestimate what they can achieve in a period of 10 years. So, I found it that a planning in 3 years just works perfect for me and for other people who seeked Plutus consultations.

Note that you do not have to fulfill only one need, but you can focus in multiple of them and find synergies. For example, you can focus on developing your family and providing the basic needs or you can focus to achieve your academic title and perhaps find your life partner in the same library...

Majority of people do not plan which need to focus on, and they let the life or other people define for them.

You had a job, you were focusing on developing your family by having your first kid, company went into cost cutting and you were made redundant. Now you need to go back to focus on your basic needs as you have no income.

It could have been avoided. As harsh as it might sound yes, it is extremely important to secure different lines of income as you need to cover the risk of any line of income might disappear.

We will go through this in detail later on in the book but it's better to understand that you need to go through pain to learn and to acquire/secure assets. You need to be willing to go through some struggles and effort as the quick and easy formula does not exist. This book will have effect on your lifestyle not if you just put the things explained in practice but also if you are willing to go through some pain in learning, researching.

Going back to our first needs, might be that other times just emergencies might arise where you have no control

- Story

Steven is getting his PHD in renewable resources in Japan. He is originally from San Francisco, CA, USA.

During the first year of his studies, Steven had a family emergency. His sister was diagnosed with kidney issues and she had to go through a risky surgical operation.

Steven knew his family would have benefited greatly from his presence from an emotional point of view. His value ranking scale scores "love" high.

Steven decided to delay his PHD, pausing his need "to learn" to focus on his need "to love". He started his studies again only after 5 months.

_____

What would have happened if Steven did not score high in the love value? Perhaps he would have continued his studies and limited to overseas videocalls.
This is exactly leading to the next chapter.

Now we move to a second aspect of your inner self, your personal values, to see how you prioritize your needs and your choices.

CHAPTER SUMMARY

SECRET 1:
Our life is dominated from four basic needs: To live, To Learn, To Love, To Leave a Legacy.

SECRET 2:
We are consciously or unconsciously prioritizing one need over the other according to different periods of our life

SECRET 3:
By analyzing your current situation, you can decide on which one of these needs you want to focus. If you want to focus on multiple needs, you need to make a clear ranking in your pursue.

CHAPTER 2

LIFE VALUES

All people are different, because their personal values are different, and they all rank them in a different way. The way people rank their own values makes a total difference to the outcome to the person that he/she is.

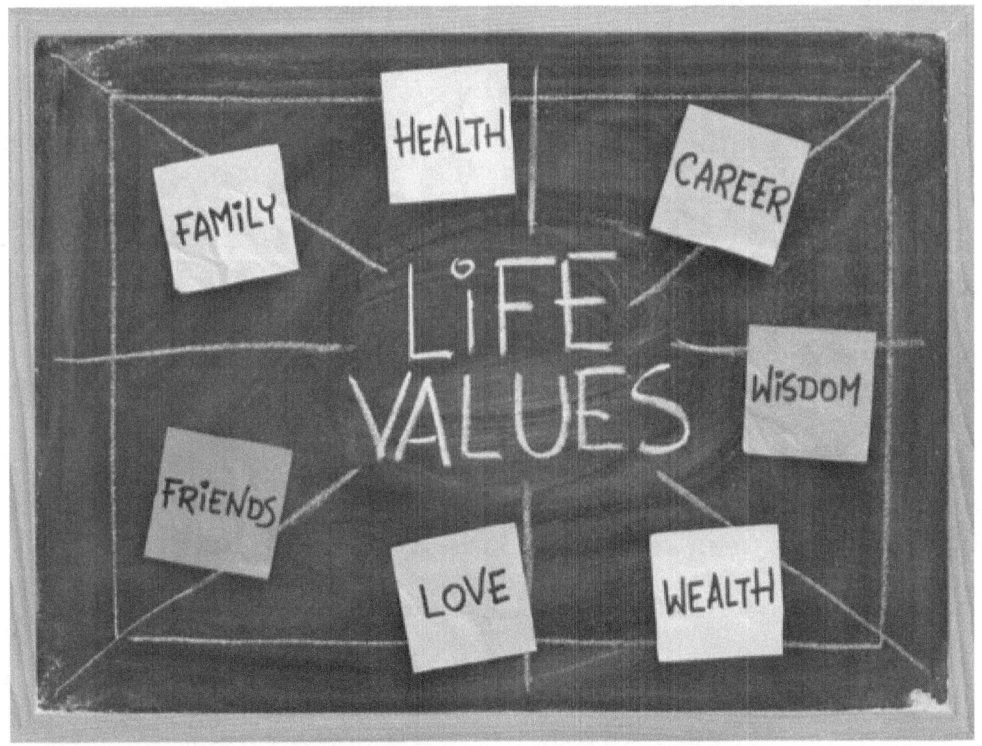

There are several values in life, to give some examples:

-Love (family): Do you enjoy spending time with your partner and your loved ones?

-Career & Success: Do you enjoy climbing the corporate ladder and feel recognized for your achievements?

-**Power:** Do you enjoy commanding others and feel comfortable by leading other people in order to achieve your (and their) goals?

-**Money:** Do you like luxury items? Do you like to visit beautiful places and fine dining?

-**Health (fitness):** Do you like sports? Do you like your physical shape? Are you concerned with your appearance and well-being?

-**Fun:** Do you enjoy games, activities and anything related to fun?

-**Adventure**: Love traveling? Love to try new experiences?

-**Freedom:** Who's taking your decisions? Who's deciding what you eat, where you go, what you do?

-**Religion & Spirit:** Do you believe in a superior force or guidance?

-**Appreciation:** Do you enjoy being recognized by others and validating those you care about?

-**Creativity:** Is imagination and creating new ideas or projects important?

-**Generosity:** If you truly embrace that the secret to living is giving, then generosity is definitely one of your values. ok

-**Self-reliance:** Being independent and not having to rely on others is paramount to those who value self-reliance.

-**Honesty:** How do you react when someone lies to you or doesn't own their actions?

-**Authenticity:** Being yourself is not being swayed by others' opinions and is vital to those who value authenticity.

People rank these values in a different way and people with a different ranking system do not get along well. Usually are the first 3 values in terms of ranking that dictate the majority of our decisions.

Let's put some scenarios together with some real stories.

John is a career focused person. John is from Houston, Texas.

John has always been busy with work where he found his greatest motivation. John is a sales manager with another 3 people reporting to him. His sales team always ranks first in the organization thanks to John efficient CRM systems and implementation of structured SOPs.

John is very successful, dedicates 40h per week to his work and 6h per week to his passion for hockey. John follows a paleo-diet consisted in eating wholefoods as he believes strongly in the proverb "mens sana in corpore sano" (healthy mind in healthy body).

John also owns 3 properties in Phoenix, 2 residentials with their own tenants and 1 commercial, used from a wing's restaurant.

His ranking of values might look like this:
1. Career & Success
2. Health
3. Money

From a cashflow's quadrant perspective, John receives income from his job (E- Employee) and from real estate (I – Investor).

Katryna is a family girl. She's originary from St. Petersburg (Russia). Her aspiration is to be a teacher since she loves kids and she like the shorter working hours and the long summer break to be with her relatives and her loved ones.

Katryna won a scholarship in a prestigious business school in France for a master in HR, given her excellent people's skills.

After long thoughts and consultation with her family, she rejected the opportunity to go abroad for a master in HR to move in different field given her excellent people skills. Katryna did not want to move away from her family and her 2 sisters so was not ready to take the leap in what could have been a career changing move.

Katryna loves cooking, especially preparing cakes and sweets. She loves to receive compliments from her nephews and she likes to experiment new culinary techniques to please her loved ones.
Katryna also manages an Instagram page for customized cakes delivery turning a small hobby in a side business

Katryna's income at the moment comes from only from the quadrant S – Self Employed and her income depends on her own ability to fulfill the orders and prepare the cakes.

So, what do you think might be her value-rankings?

1. Love (family)
2. Appreciation
3. Creativity

It is important to note that there is not such a thing like right or wrong ranking.

Now, just imagine John and Katryna meet at a bar in Moscow, during one of John's business trips.

After a beautiful night together, John and Katryna decide to meet for a second date.

Now, pause for a moment, do you see what is happening?

There is an obvious incompatibility from the beginning and you already see many problems and potential fights at the horizon. 2 peoples with different value-ranking system do not get along well as they have a completely different decision-making process.

Since we are not about couple and matching, we move on from this subject to the next example of people.

Tiago is a surfer; his hobbies are mostly related to sports in general and photography.

Tiago owns a chain of Havaianas shop in Rio De Janeiro which came from inheritance, but he does not enjoy working in it and he delegated its administration to a manager whom he pays the salary.

Tiago loves traveling in different places to try his surfing techniques and enjoy photography. He has over 5 million followers on Social media. Some people call him influencer. Tiago gets constantly contacted from surf-board manufacturers to get reviews.
Tiago is also professional on YouTube, his channel is well organized, and he enjoys vlogging.

His ranking value might look like this:
1. Adventure – love of travel and explore new places
2. Health – sport and activities
3. Fun – turning hobby of surfing and photography into small

Tiago's income come from 2 quadrants, B as business owner and S -Self Employed from his social media income and reviews.

Robert is a businessman. Robert has always had an inner curiosity and a passion to read about self-improvement and management books.

In a period of his life Robert thought that climbing corporate ladder was his goal to accomplish his financial objectives but soon he realized that it was not matching exactly his values and his personality.

Robert started early to invest in stockmarket as he wanted his money to work for him while he was going through his banking career

Robert always like to travel but given his work constrains he could not get as much leave as he wanted to.
Robert enjoys powerlifting and boxing as he likes to feel in shape and able to sustain adventures in different places.

His cashflow was coming from 2 quadrants: E-Employee and I-Investor

His ranking value might look like:
1. Money
2. Freedom
3. Health

Subsequently, Robert decides to quit his job eventually as was not providing enough freedom which was important for him. He then starts to look at different ways to fulfill his financial objectives and he starts 2 businesses, one that depends on him and one that does not depend too much on hiw activity.

His cashflow now is coming from 3 quadrants: S-Self Employed/Small Business ; B-Business Owner; I-Investor.

Paul loves to have fun. Born from mixed races, European and Asian, Paul has always been exposed to a mix of cultures both from his father and both from his mother. This led him free to choose him what to believe in as there was no predominance in the two.

Paul grew up in Singapore, a cosmopolitan city and was charmed always from gambling business. He did not like to play but he always dreamed to own a business like that, and he starts to work as an employee in the casino to learn the tricks and to have fun meanwhile.

Few years later, Paul open his own chain of online betting websites basing his company in a legal jurisdiction.

Paul also invested in a restaurant with a friend, but he has no management in it.

Paul now is living the life, with the income from his business and investment sustaining his dream lifestyle. He lives in Thailand to stay closer to his mother whom he is very attached, but he keeps on traveling and meeting new people.

His scale of value might look like:
1. Fun
2. Money
3. Love

His income is at the latest stage coming from B- Business Owner and I- Investor.

The examples above are all real people, with their names changed. Again this book want to provide facts and not fiction.
It is obvious that all the people showed above know themselves as their decisions seem to be aligned on their nature.
If you start to discover yourself is not late to align your life decisions and don't be scared of other people judgements along with it: you need to pursue your own happiness and create the financial resources to support your dream lifestyle.

This is what this book is about: **creating the financial resources to support your dream lifestyle.**

Do you know many people whom decisions are not aligned to their nature? Of course, you do!
And I bet their life does not seem smooth and happy like the people explained above.

Nida always had passion to travel and to visit new place. Nida was a flight attendant and enjoyed her job who gave her the opportunity to see the world and meet new people.
She found also her job fulfilling as she had the opportunity to help people going through long flights.

Her ranking value system might look like this:
1. Adventure
2. Fun
3. Generosity

Nida's love for her family was very high as well and her family opted for an arranged marriage as it is very strong in her own country traditions.

Nida went back to her own country and got married, to not disappoint her family.

Nida has 4 kids now and is mother full time. She still has an hobby of adventure that is now suffocated in her phantasy and she became a novel writer.

Do you think Nida is happy?
Yes, she might have a fulfilling life as she still fulfilled her needs of "Leaving a Legacy" but she needs to find soon some stimulus to fulfill her main 3 values if she does not want to fall into depression.

Keep in mind that the opposite of happiness is not unhappiness, but it is boredom: living a life without stimulus.

Exactly like the opposite of love is not hate but it is indifference.

CHAPTER SUMMARY:

SECRET 1:
Don't spend your life working aimlessly, tackling whatever job comes to hand. Have a vision for the future and align your actions according to your values to make it a reality

SECRET 2:
Take some time to define your ranking of values. Knowing them clearly might let you to better decisions.

SECRET 3:
People with a different value-ranking system rarely get along well. Knowing the ranking value of your partner and align it with yours might improve your relationship as well.

CHAPTER 3
THE POWER OF BELIEFS

According to Anthony Robbins, Values and Believes determine your decisions and your personality.

The successful stories we read in the previous chapter probably were led from empowering believes to achieve their own goals.
Let's dig into it.

Belief is something you put your faith on, what you think it is right, what is guiding you in your decisions.

There are no right and wrong believes as we live in the world where anyone can express himself or herself but there are
- Empowering Believes
- Disruptive Believes.

An example of empowering belief can be the following one:

- Jonatan has the belief that With an Ipo-caloric Diet and a Swimming Training Schedule he can reach his physical goal of 68kg and 9% body fat mass.

Do you think that Jonatan can reach his goal? Absolutely! Perhaps he will need to some adjustments along the way if he doesn't see results but with this potential belief eventually, he will reach his goal.

- Maria believes that she has a genetic disadvantage that put her fat in her lower body parts. Maria believes that she will never be able to reach 55kg of weight.

Do you think Maria will achieve 55kg body weight, even if she has the perfect diet and the perfect workout plan?

Of course not! She will find in any difficulty a support of her disruptive belief and then go back from start anytime.

Our brain works in order to support our believes, so either potential or disruptive our brain will always find support in the real world to enforce it. Our brain will find all the possible arguments to support our own beliefs.

So... where do your beliefs come from?

WHERE DO YOUR BELIEFS COME FROM?

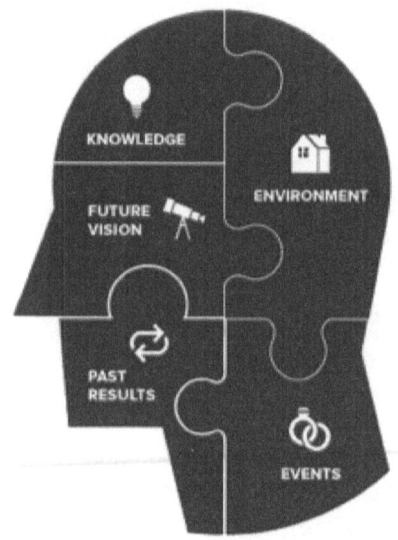

Environment

One source of believes is the environment we grow up with. This includes a mix of influences from social culture, religion, family and friends. The environment has also 30% power to determine the personality of children when they grow up.

Personality of kids is given 50% from genetics, 30% from environment, 20% from influence of parents.

Events

Especially the traumatic ones. Events impact our lives greatly as they can cause our beliefs to change unconsciously. Events can be having positive or negative impact on your beliefs.

Knowledge
Some say knowledge is power. But I would say knowledge is power if it is applied and it does not create disruptive beliefs.

Some even say there is only one thing more powerful than money, and it is knowledge.

I personally believe that a successful business needs Knowledge, Connections and Money. You may even start a business with no money at all if you have the right knowledge and the right connections.

Past Results

Everybody creates beliefs around the results of past achievements or failure. If you reach one time your physical goal of body fat 8% you will believe you can reach it again with the right methods or if you fail in a real estate investment you will believe it is difficult and it not for you and you might think to focus in another field instead.
Positive results stack up a bunch of potential beliefs, that is why it is important to try and sometimes risk. You cannot always have positive outcomes from your actions, but the important thing is that your positive results far outweigh the negative ones.

Future vision

Your imagination of the future also impacts what you believe in today. It is absolutely necessary to write down a brilliant future for you as it is the only one that you can influence. Plan your life or someone else will plan it for you.

You want your employer or the government to influence your future? You want your loved ones to influence your future? Or do you want to be the owner of your life?

Empowering beliefs help you transition into a state of being where you have absolute certainty to achieve your results. You don't just believe that you are capable, you are certain to achieve them.

As you can see, beliefs come from different sources and to create a potential belief sometimes we need to combine them.

For example, you might not believe that it is not possible to have a lifetime of income without any taxation.

And this book might tell you otherwise.
Some research might tell you otherwise (knowledge)
You start to plan not to pay taxes or minimize taxes (future vision)
You travel to a place where people have an optimized taxation management (environment)
You start to get some results of little investments where you pay minimal taxation (past results)

All this combined, will lead you to the empowering belief:

"I can achieve positive outcomes with my investments and have a minimal or null taxation"

By reconditioning your mind, you will feel empowered by confidence and positivity

"Beliefs have the power to create and the power to destroy. Human beings have the awesome ability to take any experience of their lives and create a meaning that disempowers them or one that can literally save their lives" – Anthony Robbins

I will list now some empowering beliefs that will have certainly a positive outcome in your life if you take a bit of time to think about it, support them and anchor them in your brain.

1. Failure does not exist

Every failure is a learning experience, I can get a positive lesson from this failure and get something out of it in future. Failure is just a feedback

You are scared of failure? Remember what is one of the basic human needs: to learn. Experience is not only success. Experience is a mix of success and failure and the learning that comes out of it.
If you want to learn, you need to make mistakes.
I made and lost money in many ways and many investments and each time I learned from my mistakes.
School doesn't want you to fail. Remember that school wants you to become a nice employee focuses on your primary needs and pay a lot of taxes with the promise of job security.

2. Winners take responsibility of their actions and their status

You are the maker of your life, not the government, the society, your family etc. If you are in a poor state is a consequence of your own actions so man up and stop blaming someone else.

If you make bad investment choices is your responsibility so you should not try to blame others; your brain will find comfort in blaming others for your own errors so don't fall in that trap. If you want to grow, you need to take responsibility for your actions.

Whatever good or bad in your career, business or personal decisions, is because you chose to (or you let other people influence you)

3. People are a great resource

You cannot achieve success alone. If you open a business and you don't want to spend 18h per day running it, you will need a team of trusted employees.
You might need skills that you don't have. You might need to hire people more capable than yourself. Leverage other people capabilities.
Great leaders recognize strengths not only in themselves but also in other people and find the ways to leverage them

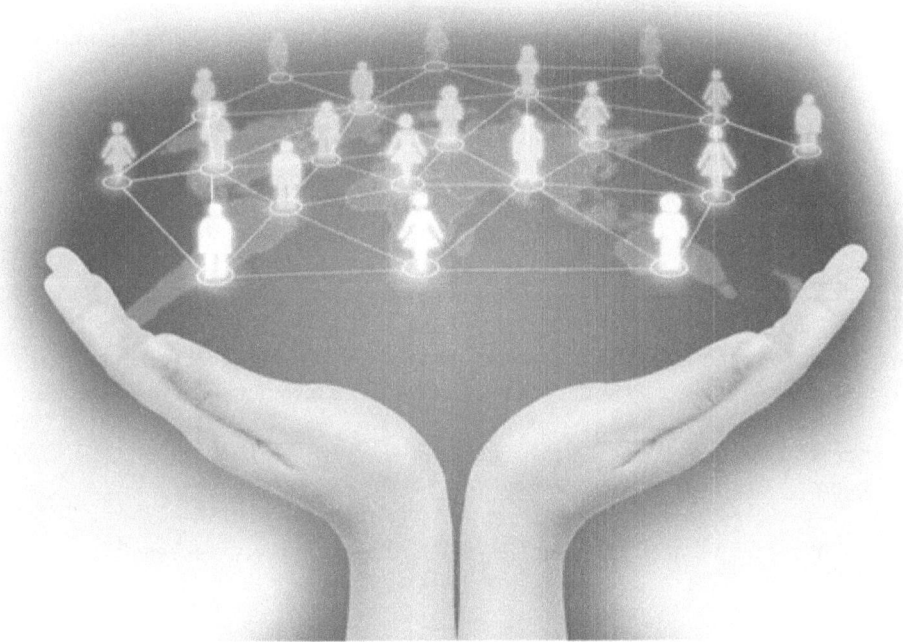

4. It is far more rewarding leveraging your strengths than patching up your weaknesses

You have an introvert-turbulent personality and don't enjoy public speaking and you always tremble by doing it, but you are a great at analyzing volatility in stock market and know the ways to profit from it.
Well, stop worrying about public speaking! It is a weakness yes, but you do not have to try to "cure it" especially if it is against your own personality (next chapter).

Instead, become an expert in volatility, you will be able to profit from it by trading options and derivatives related to it... and it can lead to an extremely fun lifestyle which is to travel everywhere in the world and trade from anywhere.

5. Work is a Game

"Choose a job you love, and you will never have to work a day in your life"

A job, a business, an investment supported from your values and beliefs and that is aligned from your personality... is not a job anymore. Is a game.
You will actually enjoy doing it.
Imagine the richest people on earth: they are still working and not laying on a hammock on Fiji island for the rest of their life. Why? Because they love working.
When you love what you do, the concept of duty time and free time will also disappear, as you will realize that both "times" will converge in only one... YOUR time.

No person has achieved success by doing something they hate.
All great inventors, painters, actors etc. they achieve success because they love what they do.

6. There is no success without commitment

It is not about how smart you are or how fast you are. It is important that you put into practice what you learn and have the discipline of following a plan to achieve your goals.

"Whatever you think you can, or you think you can't – you're right."
– Henry Ford

Tony Robbins shares a simple mental model for the relationship between beliefs, potential, action and results

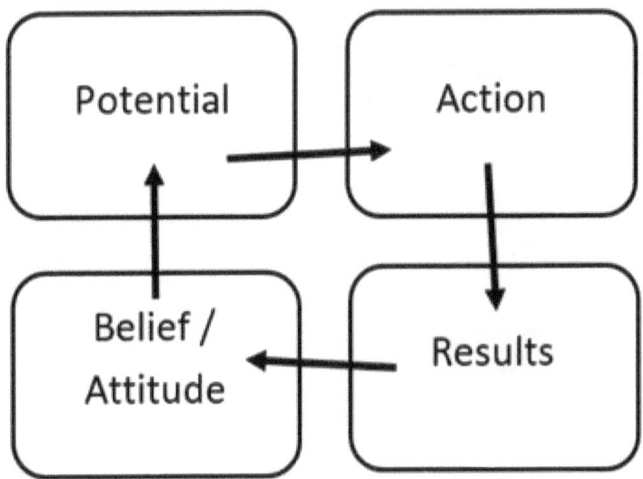

Your beliefs shape your potential, your potential determines your actions, actions lead to results that support or change your beliefs.

Your beliefs can limit or unleash your potential.

Action point:
What beliefs are holding you back?
Why you are struggle financially? What belief is there that is limiting you achieving financial freedom? Is it fear of change? Is it "the government"?

Take a moment to think about it and start to question beliefs that are limiting you in achieving your goals.

CHAPTER SUMMARY

SECRET 1:
Our life wanders about our beliefs. Beliefs leads to decisions which ultimately shape our destiny.

SECRET 2:
There are empowering, and debilitating believes. Individuating them and working on them might lead to a more fulfilling life.

SECRET 3:

It is possible to condition your mind in order to increase empowering believes over debilitating believes

After examining the needs, the values and the beliefs that guide our life, let's move to another important aspect of our inner self, our PERSONALITY.

CHAPTER 4
THE PUZZLE OF PERSONALITY

There are 5 personality aspects and combined generate a total of 16 different personality.

Some people have their entire life mapped out by the time they enter kindergarten.

But for most of us, finding our life's work takes a bit more effort, especially since career paths aren't always straightforward and predictable.

So, if you don't know what you want to do with your life, don't sweat it – just start experimenting.
This is a good strategy because careers develop in unforeseeable ways and every job or project that grabs your attention could be a step toward your true calling.

Say you follow your dream and join the circus. After a few months, you start to realize that you're not so into cleaning up after elephants. So you transfer to the box office to sell tickets, but this new job, a bit too pleasant and a bit too clean, quickly gets boring.

Done with the box office, you decide to get an office job outside the circus. Your new job is just starting to get on your nerves when you meet a client who owns a clothing line.

Suddenly you realize that you were born to design circus-themed T-shirts!

The point is, you don't need to subscribe to a seemingly established career path. While some people are staunch believers in the notion that careers do follow strict scripts, these assumptions are invariably based on other people's experiences.

For instance, a common rule is that if a career opportunity comes your way, you should seize the chance because it might be your only one. And to seize the perfect career you should find the one that matches your personality.

Remember that just because something worked for someone else's career doesn't mean it will for yourself.
That's why it's important to flip the script, that is, to rewrite traditional career advice to match your needs and your personality. You might ditch the rule about jumping at your first career opportunity and write a new one that says, "If you don't feel good about a job, pass it up." There will always be other options.

Your ideal job or business should be the perfect mix of joy, money and flow, with working conditions that match your personality.

Imagine you had the chance to make one wish and you chose to win the job lottery, but it's still up to you to specify exactly what you want.
What does your ideal job entail?

For starters, it should have the right mix of joy, money and flow. After all, the ideal job is one that pays you for doing work you love.
If working with children is your greatest joy, second only to explaining things, then being a schoolteacher is perfect for you.

But, of course, enjoying your work isn't the only important factor; there's also the issue of money. Even if you don't want to be rich, it's hard to enjoy your life if you're constantly stressed about making ends meet.
And finally, your ideal job should let you experience flow, a mental state in which you're completely immersed in an activity, forget about time and do your absolute best work. Flow comes usually only with jobs that match your personality.

All three of these ingredients are important for everyone, but the difference lies in how much of a priority each one is to any individual.
So, joy, money and flow are central to determining your ideal career, but your working conditions are too. You might love the content of your work, but if your day-to-day conditions are poor you'll just wind up stressed out and unhappy.

To prevent this from happening, it's important to determine the conditions that are right for you. For example, how important is it for you to set your own schedule? Could you be happy working a 9-to-5 job? Then consider what type of social environment suits your

needs – do you want to work solo or on a team? Do you prefer working in a shared office or at home?

Lastly, there's reporting and accountability. In other words, do you prefer working autonomously or are you fine with being managed? How do you feel about your actions being monitored? Once you've answered all these questions, you'll have a stronger sense of what kind of job is right for you. Now it's just a matter of implementing a strategy that helps you attain it!

Understand your personality will make you understand not only an optimal business/career path but will help you understand better also the people around you

You can take a free test on www.16personalities.com to know your personality. You will be surprised how accurate this test actually is.

The test is interesting especially if you don't limit yourself to your personality, but you go and read also about other personality types. This will make you understand better other people as well, especially the ones close to you.

Five Personality Aspects

Mind: Introverted (I) vs. Extraverted (E)

It has been for long time been noted that some people are reserved, quiet and more comfortable alone while other people are expressive, outgoing and sometimes out loud.

The first group engage with the world spending time alone while the second one by communicating with other people.

Generally speaking, introverts do not seek or require much external stimulation and they require less communication than extroverts. Being introvert or extrovert might influence your decisions regarding your career, your business and even your eating or drinking habits.

To just give an example statistically introverts are less consumers than energy drinks and coffee.

Introverts are more sensitive to noise and disturbance in general, while extroverts sometimes need that to stimulate their life.

Extroverts are more willing to take the lead in social situations and might be more propense to take risks, they might enjoy public speaking also. Introverts on other side prefer to make attentive evaluation before jumping into decisions and conclusions.
It has been observed also that extroverts are more talkative and impulsive while introverts are more ponderate with their actions and reactions.

Energy: Intuitive (N) vs Observant (S)

Energy determines how you see the world and on which information you focus on.

Intuitive people tend to be visionary, interested in ideas and abstractions and often fantasize about something while Observant prefer facts, concrete and observable things and the tried and true.

It is important to note that this does not influence the way they absorb information but shows how the intuitive person focus on what is possible while the observant focuses on what is real and proven.

Intuitive people make excellent entrepreneurs of startup companies while observant people make excellent analysts. Knowing if you are intuitive or observant might help you decide not only which career path to take but also what kind of business you want to start:

an intuitive person might focus on innovation while an observant might focus on improvement and efficiency.

Majority of population has the observant trait, that is why intuitive people usually get more difficulty in finding a matching partner.

Nature: Thinking (T) vs Feeling (F).

Nature determines how we make decisions and cope with emotions.
All people have feelings as they are generated from the central part of the brain called "amygdala". But there is different reaction to emotions from different people.

Nature greatly influence our interaction with other people

People with thinking attitude seek logic and rational arguments, relying on "what is in their head instead of what is in their heart". They do their best to safeguard and conceal their emotions.

Thinking people are not insensitive or cold blooded as they are having emotions the same way as feeling people however, they do their best to override their feelings with their rational logic; in fact, they focus on what can be assessed, compared and verified prioritizing logic.

Statistically, thinking people are less likely to engage in direct charitable actions however they are also more likely to invest in education for disadvantages or trying to teach poor people how to fish instead of providing the fish.

Feeling people follow their heart and care little about hiding emotions.

Advocate	Mediator	Protagonist	Campaigner
INFJ-A / INFJ-T	INFP-A / INFP-T	ENFJ-A / ENFJ-T	ENFP-A / ENFP-T
Quiet and mystical, yet very inspiring and tireless idealists.	Poetic, kind and altruistic people, always eager to help a good cause.	Charismatic and inspiring leaders, able to mesmerize their listeners.	Enthusiastic, creative and sociable free spirits, who can always find a reason to smile.

They tend to be compassionate, sensitive and highly emotional. They are also not shy to cry or to express their emotions and they rather cooperate than compete.

Tactics: Judging (J) vs Prospecting (P)

The tactics scale determines how we approach planning and how we choose between options. This scale determines our attitude towards also the structure of our own life. People with the judging trait do not like to keep their options open if not if the reason is to minimize risk in other aspects. They would rather prepare 5 different contingency plans instead of waiting for challenges to arise.
These people enjoy clarity and they prepare to stick to the plan instead of going with the flow, they are usually the kind of people that determine the flow for others.

Judging people love planning, and they are the first users of "to do list" applications such as wunderlist, they like to take notes and analyze them before taking decisions and once a decision is made or a task is crossed from their list there is rarely a possibility of reassessment.

This mentality applies as much as grocery shopping or to life goals or to investment goals like buying a house.

In contrast, prospecting individuals are flexible and relaxed when it comes to dealing with both expected and unexpected challenges. They are always scanning for opportunities and options.
People with this trait understand that life is full of possibilities. They also focus more on what makes them happy than what their parents, employers or teachers expect.
If a particular task is not particularly exciting the prospecting individual will move on to another one that he/she decided is a better option while the judging individual will prefer to cross and complete also the non-exciting task.
Judging individuals are generally more stubborn while prospective are more flexible.

Statistically, it is interesting to note that majority of extroverted individuals tend to be judging while majority of introverted individual tend to be prospecting.

Identity: Assertive (-A) vs Turbulent (-T)

This last scale affects all the others, reflecting how confident we are in our abilities and decisions. This scale acts like an internal sensor, reacting to the input we get from our environments such as success or failure, feedback from others or pressure caused by unexpected events.

Identity acts like an external shell that we wear in all of our interactions with the outside world.

Assertive individuals are self-assured, even-tempered and resistant to stress.
They refuse to worry too much, and they do not push themselves too hard when it comes to achieving goals but prefer doing so without impacting the quality of their life. Similarly, they are unlikely to spend much time thinking about past actions or choices or what ifs.

According to assertive types, what's done is done, the past is gone and what to focus on is present and future as past can't be changes and there is little point in analyzing if not to find some teaching lessons that might improve their future.

Not surprisingly, people with this trait are generally satisfied with their lives, they feel confident in their ability to handle challenging and unexpected situations. They are always surprised when other people see problems in what, for them, can be a learning opportunity or something that can be a positive event in their life if not now but in future.

In contrast, turbulent individuals are self-conscious and sensitive to stress. They experience a wide range of emotions and tend to be success-drive, perfectionistic and eager to improve. Always feeling the need to do more, have more and be more.

Turbulent types may forget how exhausting this dissatisfaction ca be – both for themselves and for the people around them.

While the assertive identity may seem more positive on the surface, that is not necessarily the case.
Turbulent individuals are more willing than Assertive types to change jobs if they feel stuck in their current roles and they think deeply about the direction of their lives. Turbulent individuals are also less likely to get in trouble with the law and to engage in dangerous activities while assertive individuals may sometime be overconfident in their decisions.

Now, there are sixteen combinations that lead to sixteen personalities with these traits. You briefly saw them in previous pages with small descriptions.

ENTJ-A
ENTP-T

Etc.

If after reading this chapter you can already come to your combination, good. If not, I suggest you to take this free test on www.16personalities.com that will tell you who are you.
The test is very accurate and will surprise you how it will show your personality in detail. It will take only 10 minutes and is recommended to do it before moving on.

CHAPTER SUMMARY

SECRET 1:
There are 15 different personalities, each person his different due to a combination of Values, Beliefs and Personality

SECRET 2:
Knowing your personality will help you choose the right career and business plan.

SECRET 3:
No matter what your personality is, do not be a victim of external circumstances. Take responsibility for your actions

SECRET 4:
Learn how to prioritize task and to distinguish between urgent and important tasks, DeTax your schedule.

SECRET 5:
Values, Beliefs, Personality make a person what he/she is.

PART II: DeTax your Body

MENS SANA IN CORPORE SANO

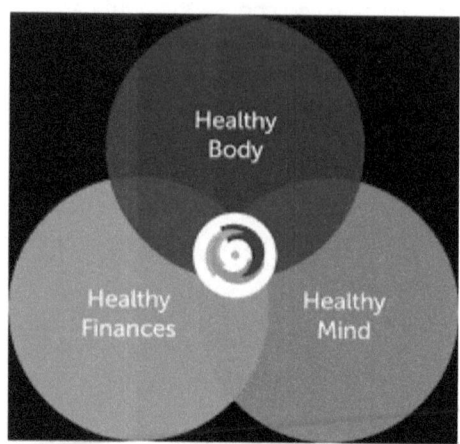

Intermittent fasting and benefits

Before moving into the technical part of this book I decided to dedicate a small section to fitness.

Even if "Health" does not score high in your value ranking systems, accomplishing your financial goals won't be possible if you are constantly sick or not in a decent shape.

Your body and mind need to be taken care of as energy is one of the main factors determining someone's success.

High performers have a positive outlook on life and are physically and mentally fit

If you were to list the habits you imagine a successful CEO might have, you might think of efficient scheduling and the ability to keep distractions to a minimum.

But you might not think of exercise.
People often associate CEOs with mental fitness, but research shows that they're also physically fit, and their energy levels tend to be similar to those of professional athletes.

Generating energy is key to maintaining a high mental-performance level.

Several scientists have found that regular exercise increases the production of new neurons in the areas of your brain that are related to memory and learning itself. Exercise also reduce stress and even improve mood. Both these factors increase your performance in your every-day work.

But everyone knows that exercise is good for you, right? Successful people stand out because they make routine exercise a habit and stick to it, while average people are great at coming up with excuses to avoid working out.

As for generating mental energy, this is achieved by having a positive outlook on life.

Data shows high performers are more cheerful and positive than their peers, even though their personal and professional lives are no less difficult and troubled. They continually and intentionally focus on the good while avoiding getting mired in negative thinking. And the research suggests that this positive thinking directly relates to high performers leading happier emotional lives and having more mental energy.

To get yourself into the habit of positive thinking, take a moment each morning to ask yourself what you planned to do for the same day. And try to squeeze some exercise in it, might be at the beginning of the day for a great kickstart of your working day for example. Remember: you need to go through some pain to get results. Here we will show some effective "pain" to go through to get good results.

Keep in mind that this isn't just about staying in a good mood: Neuroscientists believe that anticipating positive events releases as much dopamine – the hormone associated with happiness – as experiencing the event itself. Help this hormone and take in consideration what you put inside your body and how you spend your own energy.

In this way, having a positive outlook is a very powerful tool together with exercise and diet moderation. You are basically tricking your brain to put yourself on a successful path.

A healthy body is a productive body!

We all know that exercise is vital for good physical health. But if that's not enough to motivate you, you might be interested in the positive effects it has on your mental performance, too.

These effects were revealed in a study where participants were presented with color words written in a different shade of ink (for instance, "yellow" written in green). The participants then had to say either the color of the word (green) or what the written word was (yellow), before or after doing physical exercise.

The participants who solved this task after the physical exercise gave correct answers faster, showing that physical exercise enhances the brain's ability to make decisions and solve problems.

Another study found that physical exercise sharpens your focus. Here, participants were required to aim at a target on a screen while ignoring distracting stimuli on either side of it. After doing physical exercise, participants demonstrated an enhanced ability to focus and to ignore distractions.
Therefore, it might be a good idea to reserve some time to work on your important projects just after you're back from the gym. You might think you do not have time for exercise, right? Luckily, there are also certain foods that will increase your level of effectiveness too; and also remember that we always have time, but our efficiency in prioritizing how we spend this time is not always at high levels.

Regarding food, consider for instance, carbohydrates and fats: Research shows that immediately after eating carbs, you'll experience improvements in your ability to focus.

But it's short-lived, and other executive functions may decline after only one hour especially if the carbs have high glycemic index. Surprisingly, fats might be more helpful than carbs. One study showed that certain fats are likely to improve several executive functions – even three hours after eating. And beware that we are referring to nice, essential fats (EEA) here, like the ones you find in fish and nuts.

People who are dehydrated will experience more fatigue and difficulties with maintaining focus, so drinking water is also crucial if you want to lift your level of effectiveness.

An old proverb says that "we are what we eat" so keep that in mind when indulging in questionable meal choices.

And if your adventure value scores high certainly you want to have the energies to fulfill your adventurous goals.

This section wants to show you how you can reach a decent shape with a dedication of just 4-5 hours per week and some discipline when at table.

CHAPTER 1
The Efficient Dieting System

In this chapter, we are going to talk about Intermittent Fasting.

Intermittent fasting is an eating pattern where you cycle between periods of eating and fasting.

It does not say much about *which* foods to eat, but rather *when* you should eat them.

This is the preferred diet of many people in business including myself as it is proven to be efficient and absolutely the least time-consuming, time that you can spend fulfilling your goals or enjoying yourself. It might be a painful diet pattern to get accustomed to at the beginning but stay assured it will pay off. And it is far less painful than packing 8 meals per day with counted calories etc.

There are several different intermittent fasting methods, all of which split the day or week into eating periods and fasting periods.

Most people already "fast" every day, while they sleep. Intermittent fasting can be as simple as extending that fast a little longer.

You can do this by skipping breakfast, eating your first meal at noon and your last meal at 8 pm.

Then you're technically fasting for 16 hours every day and restricting your eating to an 8-hour eating window.

This is the most popular form of intermittent fasting, known as the 16/8 method and the one suggested.

Despite what you may think, intermittent fasting is actually fairly easy to do. Many people report feeling better and having *more* energy during a fast.
At the beginning you might need an adaptation period, where you can drink coffee.

Coffee is a powerful hunger suppressor and will provide you the energies to start your day. If not a fan for caffeine, you can opt for tea instead.

Time to be productive!

Hunger is usually not that big of an issue, although it can be a problem in the beginning, while your body is getting used to not eating for extended periods of time.

No food is allowed during the fasting period, but you can drink water, coffee, tea and other non-caloric beverages.

Some forms of intermittent fasting allow small amounts of low-calorie foods during the fasting period.

Taking supplements is generally allowed while fasting, as long as there are no calories in them.

If you feel hungry, focus on your work! Stay away from environments where the food is always presented to you and at home limit your grocery purchase and do not leave bag of cereals, chips etc. on sight as they will distract you and make you hungry.

A bit of theory behind it..

Why fast?

Humans have actually been fasting for thousands of years.

Sometimes it was done out of necessity, when there simply wasn't any food available.

In other instances, it was done for religious reasons. Various religions, including Islam, Christianity and Buddhism, mandate some form of fasting.

The most famous one occurs during the period of Ramadan, for Islamic religion.

Myself I experimented this type of diet 8 years ago during Ramadan, and then became a lifestyle.

Humans and other animals also often instinctively fast when sick.
Clearly, there is nothing "unnatural" about fasting, and our bodies are very well equipped to handle extended periods of not eating.

All sorts of processes in the body change when we don't eat for a while, in order to allow our bodies to thrive during a period of famine.

It has to do with hormones, genes and important cellular repair processes.
When fasted, we get significant reductions in blood sugar and insulin levels, as well as a drastic increase in human growth hormone.

Many people do intermittent fasting in order to lose weight, as it is a very simple and effective way to restrict calories and burn fat.

Others do it for the metabolic health benefits, as it can improve various different risk factors and health markers.

There is also some evidence that intermittent fasting can help you live longer. Studies in rodents show that it can extend lifespan as effectively as calorie restriction.

Some research also suggests that it can help protect against diseases, including heart disease, type 2 diabetes, cancer, Alzheimer's disease and others.

Other people simply like the convenience of intermittent fasting.

It is an effective "life hack" that makes your life simpler, while improving your health at the same time. The fewer meals you need to plan for, the simpler your life will be.

Not having to eat 3-4+ times per day (with the preparation and cleaning involved) it is also saving a lot of time.

If you sleep 8 hours a day, assuming you go to bed at midnight, you will have to essentially fast for only another 8 hours which is not something unbearable.

Water, coffee and you're good to go. You do not need breakfast; your breakfast can be easily at 4PM.

Also, with IF, you can enjoy more satisfying meals without feeling guilty.

Some people prefer to eat 3 times after their fast, other people like myself only 2 times: one big lunch and one light dinner. Be mindful that doing intermittent fasting does not mean indulging into 5,000 calories meals per time but still prioritizing high fibrous choices and whole foods when possible.

Also, after a while, you will notice a positive social outcome: you will become the guy that seems is eating a lot and not becoming fat.

However, you should stick to healthy food and limit the unhealthy choices whenever possible.

Through this diet, you can also enjoy alcoholic drinks one or two times a week, with some adjustments.

Intermittent Fasting, if followed with discipline, can be your life-hack of becoming more productive, improve your health and physical shape and also enjoy your alcoholic beverages.

Breakfast is not the most important meal of the day

This is another belief that you can add to your list of empowering beliefs.
Scientifically, breakfast makes you hungry later in the day. Your body can only benefit for a continuous fast and you will also feel more productive.

For me, as a Leangains practitioner, breakfast was a huge pain as I needed to get up earlier and I had to eat it also quickly. Also, later in the day I was even feeling hungry again. So, I start to question myself: whats the point? Why I cannot save this time?
Skipping breakfast keeps hunger away far better than eating in the morning.

CHAPTER SUMMARY

SECRET 1:
You do not need to keep your stomach always working, let it rest and work yourself!

SECRET 2:
Contrary to popular beliefs, humans can only benefit from a 16h/day fast

SECRET 3:

Whole foods and solid food options are always superior choices. Avoid super-caloric shakes and fried foods.

CHAPTER 2
FOOD CHOICES AND MACRONUTRIENTS

To have an effective diet, you need to look at your macronutrients and you need to balance them.

Calories
You need to eat less calories than what you consume to lose weight, as simple as that.
If you eat more calories than your energy expenditure, you will gain weight as your body will convert extra carbs and fats onto body fats.

Cabs and Proteins have 4 calories per gram
Fat has 9 calories per gram
Alcohol has 7 calories per gram

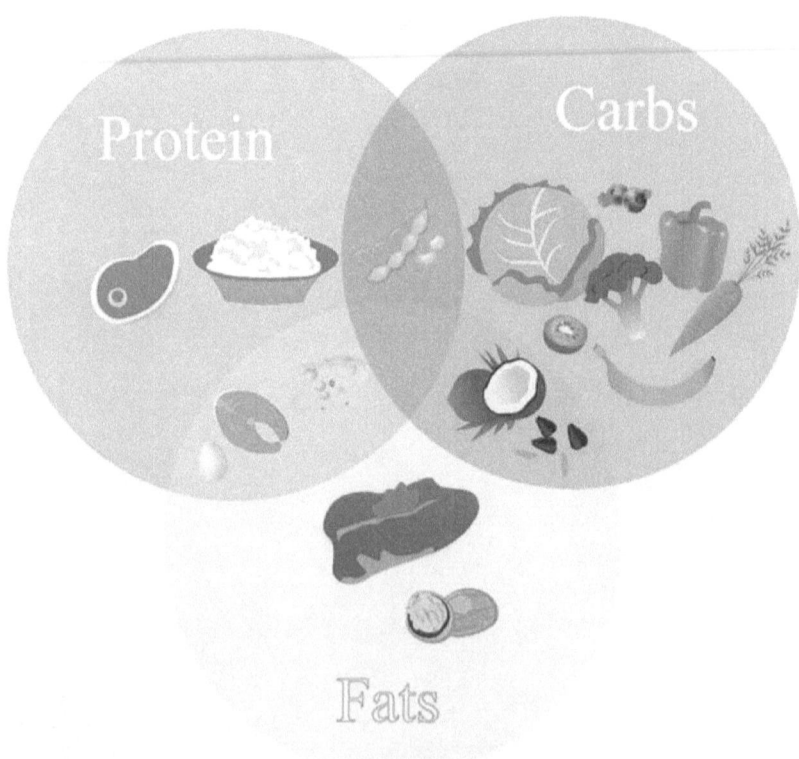

Alcohol is not included in the chart, but it also has calories, which are 7kcal per gram and these are considered "empty" calories. But is not alcohol alone that makes you fat, it is its combination with fatty food as body prioritize immediately the usage of alcohol from energy as it is seen as a toxin, while immediately any fats combined to alcohol are stored as body fat.

Your body will always prefer to convert fats into body fats as it is the easiest process, while extra carbs might be converted into body fats if they are above your overall weekly calories' expenditures.

Basically, when you are drinking alcohol your body will focus on consuming those calories, and if ingested with carbs or fats, the latter will be immediately stored.

Macronutrients

The composition of your macronutrients in your diet is also extremely important as not all calories are the same. You cannot for example live all day with drinking olive oil just because you reach those 2,000 calories.

In general:
Proteins are used to support your muscles and as third source of energy. It is very very complicated for the body to convert proteins into fats; that's why protein's only diets are usually the fastest to help achieve weight loss (although not recommended, as they carry other health problems)

Carbs are used as first source energy as they are the preferred "fuel" for the body

Fats are used from the body to secrete hormones and as a secondary source of energy

Alcohol when ingested automatically become the first source of energy as the body sees it as a toxin and wants to get rid of it as soon as possible

Protein and Fats are necessary for survival and should be present in every diet, all studies (especially the ones in keto-diets) show that we can be perfectly healthy by eliminating carbs from our diet but that would mean a great negative impact on your overall mood, so I also don't recommend a limitation but a moderation instead.

You should consume in average 1g x body weight of fat, 2g x body weight of proteins and the rest of the calories from carbs. This is an easy tool to structure your diet although I recommend following the below combination:

Workout Days

2g x body weight protein (if you weight 70kg this is about 500g of chicken and 2 cans of tuna per day)
0.75g x body weight of fats
Rest of calories from carbs

Rest Days

2g x body weight protein (if you weight 70kg this is about 500g of chicken and 2 cans of tuna per day)
1.25g x body weight of fats
Rest of calories from carbs

What if you do not want to follow a diet, you constantly traveling, and you are lazy to count calories even with fitness tools?

My suggestion is to start a planned approach at the beginning, it will give you the knowledge of foods in general. It is extremely difficult to count always calories especially if you are traveling and change places constantly, but with a general knowledge it will be your brain to do the work for you after a while.

You will understand for example that egg whites contain only protein, chicken is among the leanest meats and most of the times the foods you get from restaurants are high in fats as they use butter, ghee or oil in their cooking.

Keep in mind that without counting calories is quite difficult to achieve a specific body weight of physical shape but it can be adapted with these tricks, especially after you develop a knowledge of foods in general. This chapters will not lead you to compete to Mr. Olympia but for sure they will lead you to a healthy and good looking body.

1. Limit the fats and increase carbohydrates on workout days

This mean that on the days you go for your training you can eat a bit more starches like rice or bread or pasta but should try to limit fats (nuts, cheese, oil, fatty meats etc.)

2. Increase fat but limit carbs on rest days

This mean that now is the time to eat fatty meats, eggs, cheese etc. but overall you need to keep a low-calorie intake. For optimal results I suggest to completely eliminate carbs on days where you do not go to the gym.

With a bit of practice, you will find that it won't be too difficult to stay below 2,000 per day on rest days and around 2000-2300kcal per day on training days.

NB. Calories are calculated on the average person, if you are 2mt tall and already very muscular of course these calories will appear very low but for vast majority of people this simple rule of thumb works to achieve their desired physical shape.

Meal Choices

For simplicity about meal choices, I also suggest keeping eating the same meals. It will save you time in planning, counting and also purchasing.

The supermarket may give you plenty of options for foodstuffs, but only a small portion of them won't cause weight gain.

So stick to these three categories: main proteins (eggs, beef, pork, chicken breast or thigh), legumes (black beans, red beans, soya beans, borlotti beans and lentils) and vegetables (broccoli, cauliflower, spinach, asparagus, peas, green beans, sauerkraut and kimchi).

avoid drinking calories in the form of milk (any type of milk, especially the flavored ones as they keep adding up quickly), fruit juices, smoothies and soft drinks. Instead, you can drink large quantities of water and unsweetened tea and coffee. One or two glasses of red wine per day are also OK, but I suggest limiting alcohol ingestion to 1-2 times a week maximum to not affect your metabolism for the rest of the week especially if you are trying to lose weight.

Limit eating fruit, as many fruits contain fructose, which is a type of sugar. Tomatoes and avocados, however, are exceptions to this rule. Also berries are superior fruits options as they are low in calories, packed with good vitamins and make you also fuller.

If we'd like to eat smaller meals to lose weight, we can fool ourselves into thinking we've consumed more calories in a meal than we actually have.

That's because our eyes, not our stomachs, tend to determine how full we feel after a meal.

So, if, for example, a meal appears large, we'll feel full after eating it even if it contains relatively few calories. Armed with this knowledge, we can simply add lots of low-calorie garnishes to our meals to make them appear large enough to satisfy us, while still ingesting a low number of calories.

Also, it is important to eat slowly. Ghrelin, an hormone present in our stomach, starts working only after 20 minutes of ingesting food. Ghrelin is the hormone responsible for feeling hungry or full.

Another way we can trick our subconscious into eating less is by changing how we decide we've had enough to eat during a meal. This saturation point isn't determined by our stomachs, either, but by social and environmental cues around us, called scripts, which we usually follow mindlessly to determine when we're "full."

For example, if you're watching a movie with a bucket of popcorn on your lap, you probably won't think about whether you're really hungry anymore or not, but will follow the script you're used to following when watching movies, that is, continuously nibbling on whatever snacks are within arm's reach until you watching that movie. Your body is in auto-pilot.

Luckily though, if we're aware of these scripts, we can change them to our own benefit. For example, in the movie situation, you could bring a small serving of popcorn instead of the whole bag, thereby forcing yourself to stop eating once it's empty. You will not feel hungry afterwards, and I do not believe you will stand up in the movie theatre in front of everyone, disturbing other people, just to buy another pop-corn bag.

The human body has a wonderfully broad and intricate set of ways to convey what state it's in.

For example, if we've eaten something dangerous, we get nauseous, and if we've been injured, we feel pain.

Unfortunately, when it comes to eating, the bodily cues that signal fullness are not sufficient to stop us from consuming more food.

Why? Because it takes too long for the "stop eating" cue to reach us. In fact, it takes about 20 minutes for our digestive system to inform the brain that we've had enough as we said before.
And a lot can happen in 20 minutes: Just imagine how many soda refills or extra chips you can consume in that time.
Of course, this wouldn't be a big problem if we ate slowly, but we don't. In fact, the average person gulps down his or her lunch in just eleven minutes.
If you're similarly fast, your body never even gets the chance to let you know it's full.

So, if our bodies don't determine how much we eat, what does?

The answer is social cues – which we rely on to tell us when it's time to stop eating.

In social contests for example we would continue to eat until the last person is eating, and perhaps if we see that nobody is eating, we would automatically stop eating as well. Social contest in eating is many times observed in sushi restaurants where they would serve big platters of sushi for people to share. It has been observed that most of the times waiters and waitresses come back to the kitchen with sushi plates with only one piece. This because of part of social embarrassment that would be approaching the last piece of food.

You can trick also these social contests by eating slow. If you are the last person eating at a table where you sharing food, most likely you would not go back eating a second time and being seen as the only one "still" approaching food

CHAPTER SUMMARY

SECRET 1:
We are what we eat. A calorie is not just a calorie, but the source is important.

SECRET 2:
Proteins are seldom transformed into body fats, a diet rich in Protein makes you fuller and leaner

SECRET 3:

You may balance macronutrients according to training day and rest day for optimal results

CHAPTER 3
THE "ESSENTIALS" WORKOUT PLAN

RPT and PROGRESSION

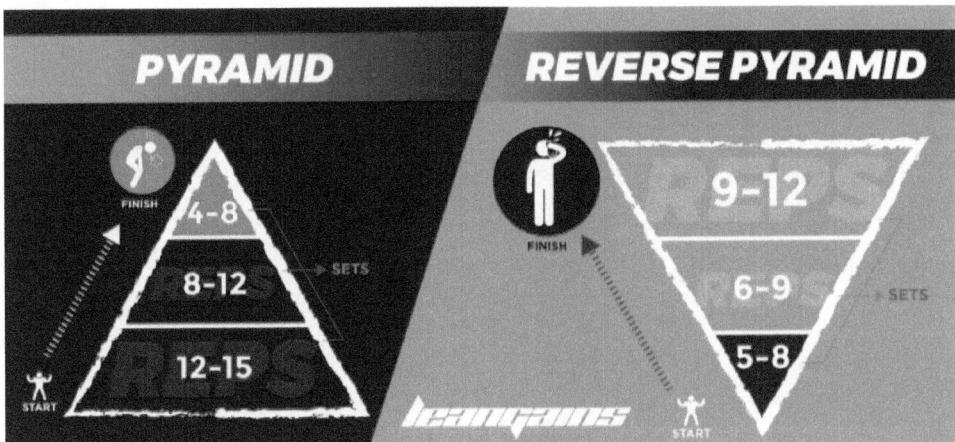

The essentials workout plan consists in a reverse pyramidal and a progression of weight and consist in visiting the gym about 3 times a week

I do not want to structure your workout even though I have a past of being personal trainer as I do not know you and I should see you first so the below are just example that might work or might not work for example if you have any specific injury to your knees or meniscus.

Like everything else, I always suggest on focusing on what takes the least amount of time and the maximum result, following the principle of *working smarter but not harder*.

Short and intense workout have been proven to be beneficial and superior from numerous studies so why you keep believing that it is necessary to go every day to gym for two hours a day?

It is not needed! To achieve result even two hours per week are enough, while I recommend around three hours per week, which includes also final cardio.

My workout schedule looks like the following:

A. Deadlift + Pullups

Deadlift 4-4-4-5-6

First 3 sets load is increasing as they include warm up, while last 2 sets the load is decreased as the reps are increased. This is exactly the same principle of RPT and it is applied on all main exercises.

Pull ups/Chin ups 6-8-10

I put overload and I start with the heaviest but if you are unable to do them you can use lat machine

Leg raise 3x15 (abs)

Cardio 10minutes

    B. Bench Press

Bench 6-6-6-8-10
Dips 4x20
Sit-up 3x20
Cardio 10'

    C. Squat + military

Squat 6-6-6-8-10
Military press 6-8-10
Crunch 3x15
Cardio 10'

I use 2 minutes of rest for the first exercise, 1.5' for the second and 30secs for Abs.

Each one of these workouts lasts between 45' and 1' so stop using the excuse that you do not have time. I put 1-day rest in between workouts and 2 days rest after Squat, so I can recover for my deadlift.

After 12 years of training is it tough for me to increase weight on the main exercise although I still try to do so as that's the way to get progress so you should do the same.

New belief for you: **"I can achieve a very good physical shape with just 3/4 hours of workout per week"**

The reality is that everyone has time, it is up to you if you use it efficiently or not so stop sitting on this classic excuse "I do not have time".

At this point you should have understood the benefits that a good physical shape has on your mind and your career as well. You do not need to compete for Mr. Olympia, but you can easily achieve a 12% body fat body while balancing your weight with your height.

This means that if you are 1,80cm tall, your optimal weight is around 80kg with 10-12% body fat.

CHAPTER 4
THE ESSENTIALS SUPPLEMENTS FOR BODY AND MIND

Below you will find a small list of supplements that are actually essentials and are the ones that will help you achieve your health and fitness goals and also provide a psychological support to your physical and mental energies.

OMEGA-3

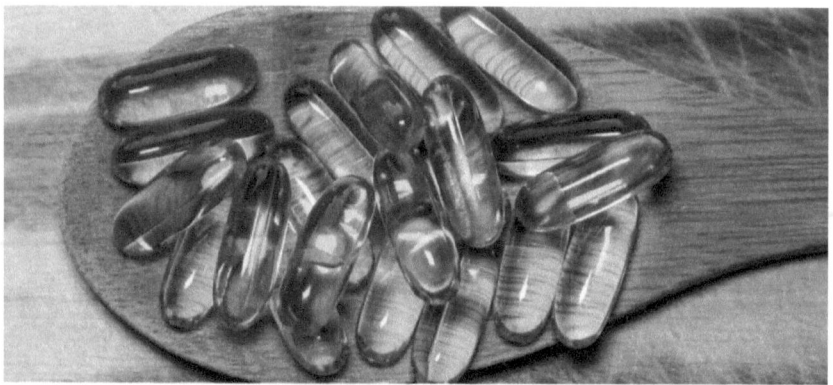

Omega 3 have positive impact on cardiovascular health, reduce the risk of atherosclerosis, debilitate Alzheimer's disease risk and diminishes risk of depression.
Furthermore, omega 3 affect development of brain functions, such as intelligence, vision and mood.

Physically, omega 3 accelerate also fat loss in some studies.

All this is scientifically supported from many studies.
Omega 3 supplements are also inexpensive, and I cannot imagine eating salmon every day either.

Majority of supplements to not yield high amounts of EPA and DHA so you might need to take above the recommended dose which is 2g EPA and 1.5g DHA per day. Now Foods is a famous manufacturer that provides cost-effective omega-3 supplements.

Vitamin D

This is essential especially if you do not get enough sunlight. Vitamin D prevents heart diseases and may boost also strength and athletic performance. 2000 IU/Day is a conservative and safe dosage

Caffeine

If you are not a regular coffee drinker, you can consider integrating caffeine pills in your diet. Caffeine is a potent hunger suppressor and a stimulant that will help you burn easily 200kcal more per day that is about 0.25kg of fat loss per week.

Calcium

This is for people that do not consume dairy. Calcium increases fat exertion and boost testosterone. Adding 500mg per day will do the trick

That's all what you need to get your mental energies and achieve your physical goals, do not waste your time reading about other supplements and do not be a victim of marketing from supplement companies.
I always suggest getting scientific backup of any supplement, that you can find on www.examine.com .

It is important to stay healthy and fit and reward yourself regularly.
Remember that a healthy body is home to a healthy soul, increases your confidence and curiosity and makes you more resistant to stress.
A strong mind has to be supported from a strong body.

Now that your body and mind is ready, we can move on to the technical side of the book.

SECRET: Only few supplements are really worth, stick to the essentials for body and mind.

PART III: Detax your Wealth

INTRODUCTION

So now you learned a bit more about yourself. You learned how to achieve your physical shape. It is time for business, right?

Now you want to make some money and you want to start protecting your wealth from taxation. This second part will be a bit of teaching a bit of autobiographic so you can take in inspirations the actions and results done from the protagonists of the various stories taken into example.

Well, let's get started: it is time to "DeTax" your financials.

CHAPTER 1
The Quadrants of Cashflow

Before moving on, it is important to notice where is your income coming from at the moment. We have already made a small introduction when we talked about values, peoples and their stories but now we will go into details.

Robert Kiyosaki created this excellent tool called cashflow quadrants. Through this tool you can have a quick and easy idea to understand where your income is coming from and where your goals should be focused.

You will also understand where traditional school and society is teaching you to be.
If you want to make change, it is now a good time to understand your starting point and also to take time to find inspirations located in the different quadrants to look up to.

E- Employee
Your income is coming from the salary you get at the end of the month. This includes also any commission, bonuses, allowances etc.

Producing income as employee is usually taught in most schools. Even business schools, very rarely teach you how to create and fund your own business but they usually opt to the easier way of teaching you how to become a good financial analyst.

Do not forget most of the times the professors themselves know only how to produce income from the E quadrant, perhaps they lack B and I experience.

S- Self Employed or Small Business
Your income depends on you, you are a lawyer or a doctor and need to declare taxes. Sometimes you find very high net worth individuals in this category, and it takes many years of studies to achieve these types of professions.

Although greatly satisfying, the only outcome is that the income still depends on the time and work you put yourself into.

B- (large) business owner
You own a business and you pay salary to other people. This is for the small businesses where the owner manages to "disappear". This means that you have your own manager, your own accountant, your own sales team to run the show. If you are in this category, you want to have minimal or limited interaction with your own business as perhaps you are busy building another business or enjoying fishing in the Fiji islands.

I-Investor
You invested in several businesses or in stock market or in real estate and you do not work with it, but your money is working for you. Here you don't have people working for you but you have your own money working for you.

Being an investor means owning shares of existing companies through either public or private equity, owning lands or apartments, or investing in commodities.

Note that E and S are the most taxed categories, so unless your value-ranking of "career" is high and you are pursuing the climbing of corporate ladder for power and prestige, I would not recommend holding this quadrant for too long.

If you are a doctor or a lawyer, you might start to plan to expand your studio and hire other people who can also replace your work to not have always your income depending on your own strengths.

I personally moved from a path consisting in starting by being a small investor and employee to owner of 2 businesses and actively investing in stock market in products like public and private equities, stocks, bonds, derivatives.

My Journey

First Phase: A tax-free employee salary

As you might think, it is not easy to start a business from zero and it is not easy to start without having enough knowledge, experience, connections and financial resources.

This is one of the choices why I chose to start my career as employee.
The objectives were simple: to learn as much as possible in sales, finance and investments and to put some savings on the side to start side businesses later on.
I needed money and knowledge basically, as well as connections.

Knowledge + Connections + Money = Business

My first job was in accounting and finance in a corporate investment banking firm.
I had the opportunity of mastering accounting and finance principles while improving my knowledge in the stock market.
I remember coming to Dubai, UAE without anything. I was just looking for job for about 2 months while doing some part-time jobs such as teaching Italian and working as private personal trainer.

One day I joined a networking event hosted from Bloomberg. In this event I met an Italian speaker Bank Director, whom introduced me to what would be my first employer in UAE.

This job was based in Dubai as well.

Why I chose Dubai?
Well, because I did not want to pay taxes on my income knowing that Employee is the most taxed category. In Dubai all Employees also enjoy tax-free salary.

Many international authors on personal finance dislike this category as they know it is the most taxed one, but I overcome to this barrier by working in UAE, where all salaries are entirely tax-free.

So... I left everyone: my family and friends and my own home country to start my new adventure in the pursue of my goals.

I kept the finance job for about three years, meanwhile I was saving and continuing my own investments in the stock market.

Starting your investment career as employee has the advantages of:

- Learning
- Obtaining financial resources
- Make connections

While the second is always dependent on your time, it means your trading your time for money, you should not underestimate the possibilities of learning new skills and making right connections which sometimes are more important than the financial compensation from your job.
This is called long term planning.

Then.. Make a Plan!

Do you want to live, or you want to exist?
Plan how long you will keep that specific job and what are your goals by doing it every day.

If you are demotivated, if it doesn't match your values or it does not provide any stimulus... change it! Do not waste your time in something you don't like.
After all, **no one has ever excelled in anything by doing something they hate.**

That is why knowing your personality and your values it is fundamental also for choosing your first job.

If you are currently an employee, and you are not working in a fiscal paradise, I am not forcing you to leave your job.
But you need to find a way to liberate yourself from the office, so you get more time to focus on your investment for future and create side businesses.

You can use the following formula.

Define your goals and eliminate all interruptions. Make it as a rule to reply to emails only ¾ times a day and not check them constantly. Your goal is to accomplish in 10 hours what your co-workers get done in 40. But remember: most workplaces encourage activity, not effectivity, which means that no matter how little time it takes you to complete your work, you'll always have to put in 40 hours per week.

The solution is to escape the office. Not only will this allow you to work less, it will enable you to work from anywhere you want.

Try to get a trial period from your boss, where you will show a great increase of productivity when you are working outside office to convince him to allow you to do so.

Below you find the steps to "disappear" from office:
1. Increase your value to the company
2. Prove increased output when working remotely
3. Quantify the business benefit
4. Propose a trial period
5. Expand the time you work remotely

Let's take a look at how Sherwood, someone who wants to dedicate more time to his side business of selling sailor shirts on eBay, pulls off this "vanishing act."

He starts by making himself indispensable. He talks to his boss about additional training that will help him serve better the company's clients, the goal being to increase his value to his employer.

In the meantime, he conducts a little test: he calls in sick on Tuesday and Wednesday and says he will work from home. These days are chosen not to give the impression of wanting to extend the weekend, and also, he does not want to be conditioned of the coming weekend either.

On these days, he keeps track of how much work he does with quantifiable records and an email trail – and he purposely doubles his work output, an achievement that is not that difficult given that he is avoiding pretty much all office distractions

Sherwood then creates a proposal detailing how his working from home will benefit his boss and why he's more productive out of the office, since he does not have to worry about commuting or common office-related distractions.

At this point, he suggests a revocable trial period: he will work from home one day per week for two weeks. The suggestion is accepted and on these at-home days, Sherwood again ensures that his productivity doubles compared to being at the office, which gives him further proof that his working from home is beneficial to the company.

Now all he has to do is increase those away days to five, which should be easy considering the added productivity his boss is seeing, and Sherwood will effectively be able to work from anywhere in the world and get the time he deserves to cultivate his side business.

Second Phase: Opening Side Business

So as you might have understood in my first job I was trying to limit my time in the office by convincing my employer to be more productive remotely, as most of the times I had to reconcile statements or upload them in the accounting system so it was something it could have done easily remotely.
I did not manage to disappear from the office entirely, but I was quite close by reducing office working hours and adding a day per week of remote work.

In my first job I was also trying to make connections, put savings on the side and expanding my knowledge. And at certain point something interesting happened

For my 24th birthday, I booked a yacht in Dubai, UAE to celebrate on it with friends. Booking a yacht is a great opportunity to see all Dubai skyline and enjoy a nice party with music, food and drinks with the people of your choice.

I really liked the cruise and I started to get curious about this business as I was still undecided what business to start so... what if I could start something "fun"?

I started to do some research, I spoke with a couple of friends and after 6 months we founded "Neptune Yacht Rental LLC".

Company has jurisdiction in Dubai Mainland as it offers B2C services.

Neptune is a yacht charter company, so this looked like a little dream of owning yachts and use them also for personal leisure, while conducting business activity with it.

The yachts became also my favorite networking platform.

Through weekly parties I invite key people either to develop the yacht business such as travel agents, event promoters, party organizers, wedding planners etc. but also to connect with businesspeople in other fields.

I soon realized that work can be fun too, and you can do it as well.

I left my job in the brokerage company when I decided to dedicate myself to this new business, only when it was profitable enough to cover at least my most basic life expenses.

Second -half Phase: The Pizza Place Failure

This is when our yacht company was growing, and as a promotion we launched an interesting pizza-yacht combination. Basically, we were giving free pizza to our client to all weekday bookings when they book a yacht.
This promotion was quite successful, and we partnered with a pizza place on purpose to deliver pizzas to our yachts right before the customer's trip would start.

After a couple of months, my idea was to have a second synergic business with the yachts, and I thought: why not owning a pizza place as well? It makes perfect sense on paper right?

So me and my partner acquired a small 500sfqt pizza place, in a great delivery location but with very small footfall.

I realized quickly that the orders from the yachts were not enough to sustain the pizza place. The location of it was not great, our online presence was scarce, my own time to dedicate to the store was very limited and the employees were unruly. We lost a bit of money in this place but eventually we managed to sell it. I learned the hard life of restaurant owner and I learned that it requires a lot of time to manage it well and the high fixed costs require a very high volume of dishes to be sold to breakeven.

Third Phase: Government Job

After few years of the yacht company, which grew from one to two yachts, I was approached from recruiter to go for an interview for a government role, in business and company setup.

I was already familiar with the process of opening company and I thought that this could have been a great opportunity also to meet new investors that perhaps could have had interest to join an investment in the yacht company to expand it.

I decided to take the job. At this point my income was being produced from 3 quadrants:

E- Government Employee Salary
S- Small Business Owner
I- Stockmarket investments

Forth Phase: Going solo with own investment company

After few years, more savings, more connections... the yacht company expanded to a fleet of 4 yachts and more employees, making the income deriving from it moving from S-Small Business to B- Business Owner.

I decided also it was time to leave the employee life, at the age of 29, to prioritize my freedom to work whenever and wherever I wanted.

That's 2019, and Plutus Financial Protection LLC was born.

Through Plutus, I get the chance to give back to society. By showing how to create efficient tax company structures, residences, citizenship and related alternative investments.

Plutus has the aim to help people protecting their wealth, so they can focus on what they love by having less worries, less taxation... and an earlier retirement.

Now again I produce income from 3 cashflows quadrants:
S- Small Business (Plutus)
B- Business (Neptune)
I-Investor: Stock market, derivatives, funds and alternative investment in super cars.

Time for you to exercise a bit.

Where are you producing your income?
Are they from which quadrant?

What are you doing to generate income from B and I quadrants?
Keep in mind that you need to generate passive income to generate wealth and protect your freedom, and passive income comes only from B and I quadrants.

I shared my story as just a benchmark, you should not do exact the same things as my actions might not match with your values and personality. But you can take them as example and perhaps be far more successful.

Again... make a plan!

Plan what kind of pain you want to go through.
It might look all roses and flowers, but my journey was quite rough.

At the beginning of my businesses there were many difficulties in finding clients, trusting stakeholders and suppliers and to create an effective marketing strategy. I was working more than eighteen hours a day between employee, business owner and investor.
But I actually enjoyed it. You do not need to be in love with the result. Everybody wants to be rich and successful (even if they rank it low in their value system, they still want it) but not everybody is willing to go through the sufferance of hard work, risks, worries, rejects, failures and hard study. Your network might not even support you, you will feel down and demotivated but that is when you start to understand the fun of life itself... you will need to go through the pain of hire and fire people and you might have some failures and disappointments along the way but... if you have fun solving problems you are on the fast-track to success.

Start to study investments to make your money work for you.

Start to study how to create a company and what are the first steps to do to make it profitable and to make it automatic as soon as possible.

You can always book a FREE consultation with Plutus to check in your specific situation.

CHAPTER SUMMARY:

SECRET 1:
Every person produce income in different quadrants, a combination of multiple quadrants makes you wealthy.

SECRET 2:
Your resources are time, knowledge, money and network. Use them wisely

SECRET 3:
Plan your steps and do not live your career-life passively

CHAPTER 2
Build and DeTax your Personal Network

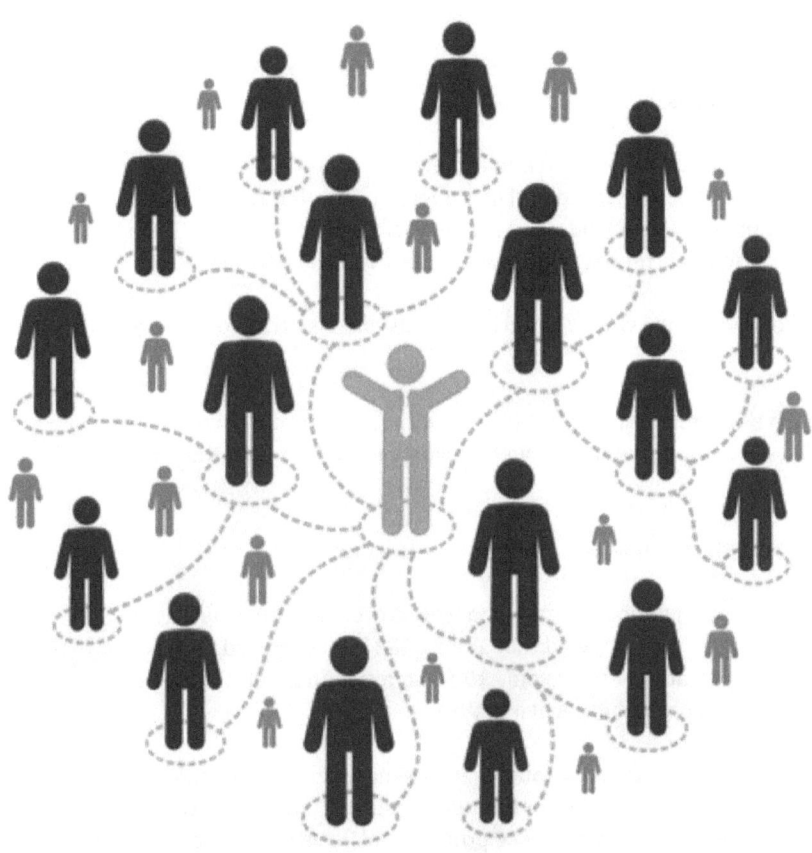

Having a personal network is fundamental for a successful career and a successful business. No matter where your cashflow is produced, your personal network can help you find a job, expand your profession, grow your business or access to interesting alternative investments.

Maybe you left dirty clothes in the washing machine, assuming your partner would hang them. Maybe you accidentally cut someone off in traffic or maybe you just did not take the time to call your father.

Yes, being selfish is normal. However, if you want to form meaningful and productive relationships, you have got to fight those selfish tendencies and nourish an important lever of success: sacrifice.

Sacrifice means putting aside your ego and focusing on others in order to create long term productive relationships. It's about focusing on collaborative work and putting aside ego.

We are all dependent on other people to achieve our goals and realize our dreams. Rarely someone can become successful in the long term without thinking about others and gaining their support. Myself I did not start the yacht business alone, but I did it with other two people, and soon partnered quickly with strong referral partners.

Sooner or later, every lone wolf will reach his limits and his career or business will come to a standstill.

Trying to build a successful career or business without a strong network is like building a house on the sand. Your foundations will weaken over time, and in the end, you may find yourself sinking.

But what is it exactly that makes a network so important?

Personal contacts open doors, increase finances, protect wealth. One classic study, outlined in the book "Getting a Job", showed that among 282 men surveyed, 56% found their jobs through personal contacts, whereas only 19% had found their job through advertisement and 10% through application of their own initiative.

Myself I got my first job in Dubai through personal network, I attended a networking event hosted from Bloomberg, where I found someone from his own home country that referred me to his friend that was hiring a finance professional in his brokerage company.

It is precisely in times of economic downturn, with their high employee turnover and high job insecurity, that having a personal network is more important than ever. People who are good networkers rarely have any problems finding jobs and customers.

Anyone can learn the art of networking, no matter how much introvert your personality is. We all fear rejection, some people more than other, but this fear can obstacle us to approach others and hence build a supportive personal network.

Some people are just too proud to admit that they may need other people to overcome to their difficulties.

Fear of rejection is familiar to all of us and you should not be ashamed of it. Few of us are natural networkers with the courage to approach any stranger to try to win them over.

There are a few tricks that can help even the shyest among us take that first big step:

- Learn from the best. Simply take notes on how an expert networker approach other people and try to replicate his/her behaviors
- Take some classes on communication and engage in professional networking organizations that promote public speaking: overcoming the fear of public speaking will help you overcome also the fear to approach strangers

You can start to target to connect with a new person per week, does not matter in which field. And have a correct mentality to network.

A good networker does not approach others by thinking "how can they help me" but instead have the mentality "how can I help others?".

The more ready you are to give, the more you will receive. Generosity builds trust and mutual understanding. This kind of behavior of giving will later on give its fruits. By giving you can expect to receive in the short or in the long term. You should not rush.

We should not see each relationship as a short-term investment and expect to have favor returned quickly. Relationships are more like muscles: they grow and strengthen the more you use them. And the more seeds you implant (i.e. the more referrals you give to other people for example) the more you will get.

People who are neither generous nor helpful, who simply aim to get rid of their brochures or business cards and only try to sell themselves or their product/service will not get much success in networking. When meeting another person, try to show interest in what they are doing or what they are involved and immediately try to connect with what you are doing and how you can be helpful to THEM.

In order to move beyond a self-centered view, and to truly strengthen and deepen your relationships with the people in your network you need to show constant loyalty to them. Loyalty can take many forms, for example, by showing emotional support to a friend who is going through tough time, or by sharing the skills you learned in this book about tax minimization.

Remember that a good networker builds a network before needing it. You should not start to look for a network when you are in the need of clients, professional advice, support etc. This is unfortunately a common mistake.

Good networking consists of following the exact opposite, you should approach people before needing their help. Doing so allows you to build trust and mutual understanding. Nobody would like anyone just there approaching others to try to get his own advantage and you should also get rid of this type of connections.

A good networker is very patient and builds a network one step at a time.
Bill Clinton followed this simple rule since he was a child. As a 22-year old stipend, he had already started his habit of sitting down every evening to write down the names of all the people he had met that day. He was always friendly and approachable to others, he kept his humility and showed interest in what other people were involved in. He ensured that he built relationships based on trust and mutual understanding, thereby creating his future network at the same time.

By building a network, you should also try to include some super-connectors. Super-connectors are people exposed to many other people, such as a barman or a restaurant owner or a club manager. This kind of people have a lot of visibility and by including them in your network you can stay sure you can share some of their visibility too.

Also, taxes might exist in your own network.

Many of us have poisonous relationships and should try to get rid of them as soon as possible. Like you may have depowering beliefs, or extra body weight, or extra financial taxation, you may also have connections who are not bringing any positivity in your life and take money and time away from you. A monthly review of the relationships with the people whom you spend majority of your time with, might pay off in the long term.

CHAPTER SUMMARY

SECRET 1:

Successful network is based on generosity and loyalty so you should always look suspicious to connections who contact you only when they need something.

SECRET 2:

A good networker builds her network before he/she really needs it, so people who approach you only when they are in need should not gain the privilege to be part of your network.

SECRET 3:

You should go periodically through your network, and a good way to do so is through LinkedIN where most of us use for professional relationships.

Remember that LinkedIN is not like Facebook and can be used successfully for network. Look for the key people in your specific field and try to connect with them; while at the same time be aware of the high variety of salespeople you can find on this platform.

CHAPTER 3
The categories of Assets

After examining the quadrants generating your cashflow is time to start to check about the category of assets, for you in order to start your investment career and perhaps move to the I quadrant.

You cannot depend only on your time to generate income; you need to start to make your money work for you. In this chapter we are going to focus on passive income, comparing to active income.

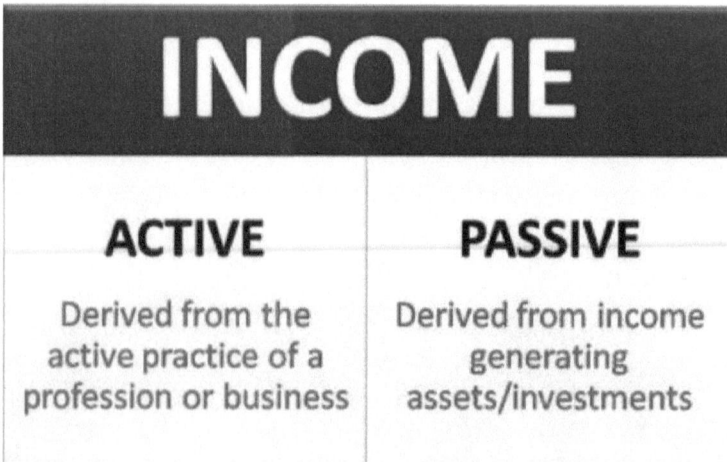

Asset is pretty much everything that generates passive income for you, which is income with minimal or null effort.

This means that to increase your wealth you need to own as many assets as possible.

Owning assets not only increases your income but protects yourself and your family from future difficulties as well.

Remember that even having a job does not mean being safe, as also by being an employee you are indirectly facing business difficulties. What do you think happens if the company you work for faces a crisis? They will need to cut expenses... and those expenses might include your own payroll.

Owning assets and securing several lines of income will reduce your overall lifestyle risk too. Protect your lifestyle, own assets, secure your assets in a minimized taxation jurisdiction.

Assets VS Liabilities

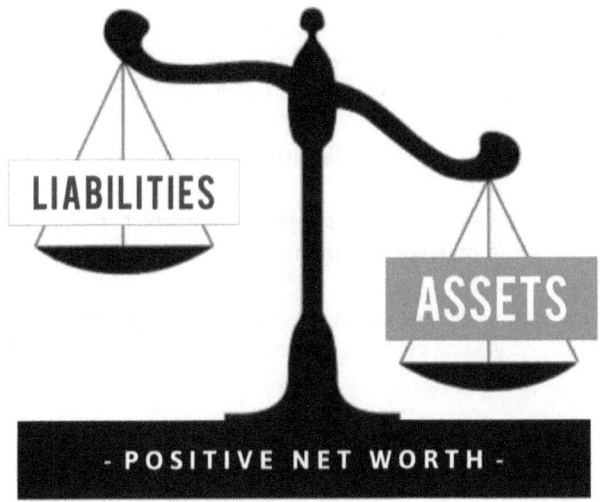

Knowing the difference between an asset and a liability is necessary to ensure you're making strong investment decisions and you are protecting your wealth.

Quite simply, an asset is something that makes you money, while a liability costs you money. An asset is putting money in your pocket while a liability is taking money from your pockets.

Clearly, it's more likely you will become wealthy if you invest in assets and avoid liabilities as much as possible.

What kind of Assets you should invest in?

Categories of Assets are three.

- Paper assets: Stocks, Bonds, Derivatives, Mutual Funds
- Real Estate: Commercial or Residential that you rent to a tenant
- Business: Any participation in running business activity, private equity, venture capital

When you invest in assets, your money becomes your 24/7 worker to create income for you. The more workers you commit, the bigger the output of their work will be.

The goal is to get your income as high as above your expenses as possible, and then to reinvest the excess income into your own assets by expanding a current business or in new assets for some diversification.

It might be difficult and scary at the beginning, but if you want the result you need to put some commitment it. You can either study the assets yourself or you can book consultation, or you can read books, or you can attend seminars or better if you add a mix of all of them. Remember, if you don't get interested yourself in this nobody will for you.

There are no right and wrong assets, and one category is not more performing that the other.

Of course, it depends on how much capital is invested and which investment techniques are used as it is possible to either make or lose money with either of them.

If you want to become wealthy, figure out what asset class works best for you, then research it, find mentors, book consultations with people with experience in that field, and acquire your assets.

Unfortunately, many people still mix liabilities with assets. This is a very expensive mistake.

Ah... the house where you live in is not an asset. It is actually one of the biggest liabilities you can have. Buying a house often means working half your life to pay a very long-term loan and perhaps having to pay also property maintenance charges.

Assets is something that creates positive cashflow for you at the end of the month.

So, the house you live in is something that you are paying with a mortgage perhaps, and it cannot be considered an asset.

Better live by renting apartment and not owning it: it makes much more sense to own apartments to rent them to others and having a rental income superior to mortgage rate. And if you have a specific residence you will not even pay any taxation on this kind of income.

The house you own and live in is not an asset because it guarantees you to have a massive expense taken away from your income every month for the next 360 months. And those 360 payments could have been invested in potentially more lucrative assets, like stocks or real estate you rent to tenants.

Also, owning your own house reduces greatly your mobility and having a high mobility nowadays is an asset by itself.

I personally have experience in all three assets category, but I prefer alternative investments as they can generate not only financial benefits but also expand your network and knowledge.

Success Story

Frank had a restaurant back in his home country, Italy.
Frank was tired of having to deal every month with enormous bills, and taxes. No matter how much his customer database was growing, he found himself paying more and more taxes.
Frank then decided to open a restaurant in Dubai, UAE.
Now he not only had the competitive advantage to offer a product which was not very common in the country, but he stopped to pay taxation.
He opened a Mainland LLC company to do so.
After his restaurant business grow, he decided to opt for an alternative investment in private equity, in a supercar rental business.
Now Frank not only enjoys income from 2 quadrants: business owner & investment, but he also enjoys driving supercars... and without paying for them.
Frank has residence in UAE, so this means that he can easily send funds in his home country, Italy, without incurring in any taxation.

Paper Assets: This is the first category of investments I started.

The investments I prefer are the ones in stocks and options.
I always liked fundamental analysis by looking at the financials of listed stock market companies and I usually prefer a stress-free investment strategy which includes picking investments in stocks with a high dividend yield and a low price/earnings ratio.
I also do not like stressing over high volume trading, so I prefer a more relaxed and long-term approach. I do not look at my investments every day but I either put stop loss and take profits, which are automatic orders once the stock price reaches a certain level, or I just sell them myself if I feel like investing in something else or if I reach a decent return on that investment (like 20% or 30%) in relatively short term.

Options give you the benefit of leverage

As most brokerage accounts are personal is it fundamental to **have residence in a place with a favorable fiscal jurisdiction** not to pay taxed on your hard-earned paper assets investment income.

Keep in mind that in most jurisdiction you have to pay taxes on the income you produce but if you lose you will not get any "refund" for your loss.

So why paying taxes in the first place?

Get a citizenship/residence "DeTaxed" first, then you can do your investments in the stockmarket.

Meanwhile, most brokers allow you to get a paper money account that you can use to practice and do some investments.

Showing investments strategy and methodology are outside the purpose of this book so if you want to focus on that I suggest booking a consultation with Plutus to expand this topic.

Keep in mind that your profession pays the bills, but your business and your investments are what will make you wealthy.

Most people consider their profession and their business to be one and same thing. You saw from the story before that Frank passed from being a small restaurant owner to an owner of a different alternative investment that brings him even more wealth.

Your profession is whatever you do 40 hours a week to pay the bills, buy groceries, and cover other living costs. You are basically focusing just on your fist need: to live.

Your business, on the other hand is what you invest time and money in order to grow your assets.
To achieve and protect wealth you must build business and invest while working at your profession. When this starts to happen, you will notice that your assets, and not your profession – become your main source of income. And when that happens you become financially free to choose to work instead of "having to work".

To make the most out of your investments, diversify.

You should invest in different categories of assets simultaneously in order to protect yourself from varying degrees of risks. The old saying of "don't put all your eggs in the same basket" still applies.

You should have an investment portfolio that includes low risks assets, medium risks assets and high risks assets. Keep in mind that are the high risks assets that potentially can change your life, while the other two categories can be considered as a safety net.

Remember also that is not possible always to earn money. Investing is a game of making and losing money and myself I know it well when I lost over 10,000EUR in a pizza place that turned out to be a complete disaster.
If you start investing, you cannot expect only to make money, but you need to consider that you will lose money too. Take it as a learning opportunity without giving to it too much emotions.

You should take advice from smart investors to guide your path, but only trust investors who have a personal commitment towards that specific investment i.e. your financial advisor should have invested himself in that product otherwise he/she is just a bank employee who is making commission out of your initial investment deposit.

CHAPTER SUMMARY

SECRET 1:
There are 3 categories of assets: Paper, Real Estate, Business. Recognize them and start investing in them to make your money work

SECRET 2:
Investing is a necessary step to become wealthy. Your profession and a traditional taxation system can only take you that far but not beyond

SECRET 3:
Combine different assets category to diversify your portfolio. A good diversification is sufficient with 6 different investments and can reduce your overall risk while improving the profitability of your portfolio.

SECRET 4:
Do not take advice in what to invest from people who do not have direct experience and results

CHAPTER 4
Personal Financial Management 1.1 & How to Reduce Personal Taxation

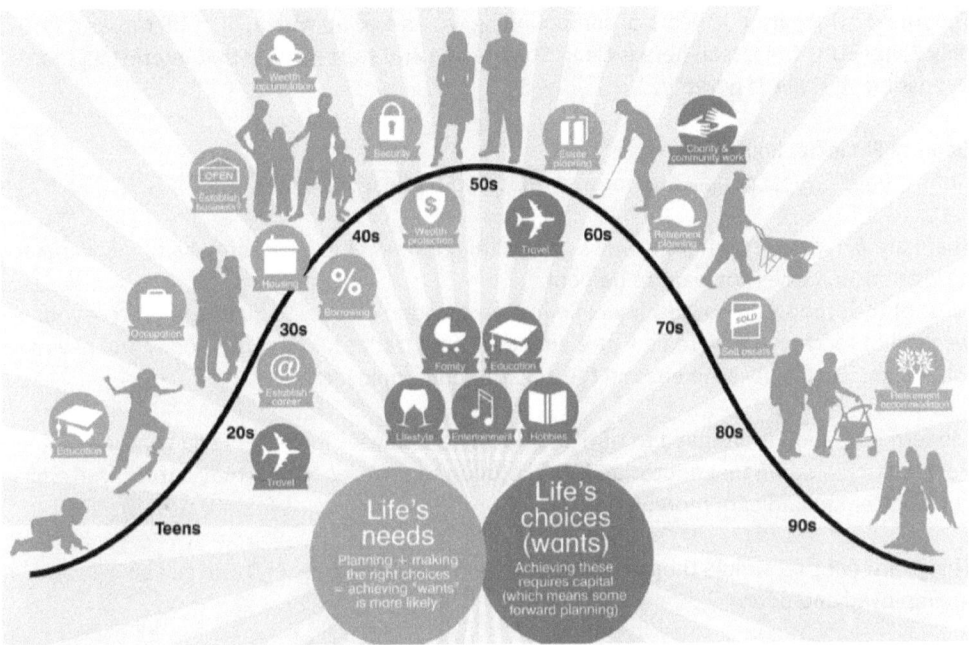

Financial Stability. To say that everyone wants it would be to point out the obvious. But too often it can seem like a distant dream. In reality, the desire to have enough money to lead a comfortable life is very fulfillable. It's also a lot easier to achieve than you think.

Healthier finances start with understanding the word "saving"

You don't have to be a financial advisor to know that no two earners are the same.

That means that financial advice is never universally true. However, there are some simple rules that apply to everyone, and it's these general principles you should follow – if you aren't already doing so, that is!

Before we get down to business, let's cover one of the basics: compound interest. Saving money makes sense only if you can take advantage of the financial magic called compounding.

So, say you have savings of 1,000 EUR earning 6 percent interest every year. Without compounding, you'd only receive 60 EUR interest every year. You'd only get up to 2800 EUR after thirty years.

But thanks to compounding, the interest you earn each year gets added to the base savings amount. It's from this new amount that your next year's interest is then calculated.

That means that, after 30 years of compounding, you'd end up with 5,743 EUR rather than only 2,800 EUR. The lesson here is clear. Start saving and start earning that interest as soon as possible. It really is worth it.

General Financial Education

Unfortunately, most people are not well-educated on financial issues.

There are a number of different views of wealth, but one thing is for sure: everyone wants to be wealthy and does not want to be poor.

Most of the schools do not teach you financial education on how to build and protect your wealth but teach you how to be a nice employee that trades his time for money and pays a lot of taxes for the government and the government employees.

Modern education is designed to turn people into employees, taxpayers and consumers. People often assume that education is the solution to poverty: if you study harder, you will get a better job and earn more.

Things are not that simple though. You can have master's degree, PhD and still be unemployed and poor.

Just try to remember a simple equation for a successful business or career:

Knowledge + Money + Connections = Success

There is certainly nothing wrong with being a hard-working taxpaying consumer, but that alone won't make you wealthy.

Schools don't prepare students to make money in the world, schools don't offer any sort of financial education. So the Knowledge component coming from schools it is quite limited and "controlled".

Schools do not teach you how to make money, do not offer trial of trading platform in stock market, do not offer seminars hand to hand with entrepreneurs. This means that schools do not teach you how to make money but teach you how to pay taxes instead.

Even business schools sometimes fail in the purpose of trying to educate their students to successful networking practices. Networking events are usually only encouraged and sponsored by business schools but again their aim is to connect you with potential employers, not to build lifetime relationships that can enhance your customers' acquisitions, your financial management and your marketing strategy.

Remember that to become wealthy you need knowledge, money and connections.

Knowledge can be nurtured with books, seminars, consultations, mentors, alternative education, internships etc.

Money can be made with fundraising for your startup, angel investors or your other investors and minimizing your taxation impact.

Connections can be made with right networking attendances and practices.

How to manage financial crises?
Again, schools leave many people defenseless against financial crises. For example, most people think the 2007 crisis was a stock market crash, but it was actually a derivatives market crash caused from subprime mortgages. That is, banks directors were playing with taxpayers' money by creating poisonous derivative instruments that they sold later on to the same taxpayers' money.

Derivatives are complex financial instruments that look like insurance policies... but in reality, became hot potatoes as financial institutions was selling them as soon as possible as the underlying assets were fading.
They can be seen as the equivalent on "betting" on the stock market.
Of course, not all derivatives instruments are bad and quite few of them are effective in building and protecting wealth but a in ignorance in their purchase might lead to substantial losses.

If the population had better financial education, they might have known the increase in the derivatives market between 2000 and 2007 presented big risks and would eventually cause the crash.
And they would be better equipped to face similar problems in the future.
Most probably they had mistaken derivatives for assets... while derivatives are mostly an instrument for speculation or protection.

Having a low financial IQ brings also to make confusion between rich and poor people and make stereotypes. Many people mistakenly assume that wealthy people are evil and purposefully make others poor.

In some cases, there is truth to that, but not always. Some people become wealthy precisely because they are generous and they want to contribute value to the society: by presenting products or services that increase the overall wellness of the society, by creating new jobs and by even founding charity organizations on a later stage.

John Rockefeller was one example. He became rich by selling petrol at cheaper prices than any of his competitors, which also made life much easier for millions of working-class people who did not have access to petrol before.

Yes, there are also a lot of rich people that become rich with illegal businesses and practices. Ponzi and his scheme was certainly one of those but as there are good and bad rich people there are also good and bad poor people so if stereotypes might give you a general guideline about how to think about a specific subject, they need to be treated carefully as they are not always right.

You cannot become wealthy without adequate financial education.

When people say you need to be educated to be wealthy, they usually mean you need to get a university degree. What you need actually is financial education that includes expanding your knowledge, your assets and your network.

School don't teach financial education because is too powerful.
Financial education means looking beyond traditional explanations and gaining the **knowledge and the network necessary to create more assets and pay less taxes.**

In the past, slaves were not allowed to learn how to read and write, because it would have given them more power over their owners. These days, most people are deprived of financial education for the same reason.

Real wealth is not about getting a high salary, that is another misconception. It's about having assets that put money in your pocket without having to work for them much.

It's about knowing the legal structures to minimize your taxation; it is about getting in the mindset of correct management of your spending power.

You might think it's easy to determine whether someone is rich or poor but it's not actually that simple. Appearances are not always right, and perhaps a person can even be poor if he lives in an expensive house or drives a luxury car.
Do you know if someone is renting the car or he bought it? Do you know if someone is living temporarily on-debt in that luxury house across the street?

If you want to change your financial situation, you first need to know where you stand. And having padronance of your income statement and balance sheet is one of the chosen personal financial management best practices.

David is a renowned plastic surgeon. His profession brings him over EUR 10,000 per month. David lives in a villa which he pays EUR 3,000 per month, he also owns a Ferrari which he pays another EUR 2,000. David is still left with EUR 5,000 which allow him to have a wealthy lifestyle.

David has no assets: no apartments rented to tenants, no stocks, no alternative investment in private equities, no royalty from manuals he wrote.

So, what happens if one day David gets sick and cannot perform his profession?
Try to imagine that. He still will have to pay for his house and his car and probably he will have to sell them both. His wealth is not protected at all and he does not have diversified sources of different types of income.

Having a profession or a job does not protect your wealth, your assets protect your wealth and your residence or company structure protects you from paying too much taxes. Sometimes taking risks mean reducing other bigger risks.

Thinking about rich people as those who eagerly spend in luxurious goods or show off constantly is another misconception.

Remember that many millionaires don't live the high life. They budget wisely to maintain their affluence.

If you were a millionaire, you wouldn't hesitate to wear Gucci and drink Champagne every day for dinner, right? Sorry to destroy your stereotype, but many rich people have a very simple lifestyle and they are careful with the money they spent.

If you want to DeTax your financial life, you have to learn to take responsibility of the wealth you generate.

If you are born poor it is not your mistake, if you die poor it is your mistake.

The majority of self-made successful businessmen have modest backgrounds and achieved great wealth by saving their monthly earnings and avoiding spending cash on stuff they didn't need. The simple rule is one way you too could become a millionaire, without ever actually making a million dollars a year.

People increase and protect their wealth by controlling their budget and maintaining their affluence in the same way. They are also practiced at thinking long term and planning for the future.

A survey of millionaires found that for every 100 millionaires who were not budgeting and thinking about their financial future, there were 120 millionaires who certainly were.

Planning and structuring expenses is key if you want to grow your wealth.

Mr. and Mrs. Proietti are millionaires, and their main goal is to be financially independent when they are ready to retire. By this time, they want to have saved EUR 4 Million.

To make this happen, the couple cleverly allocates their time and money so that they can continue to invest in their business while earning and saving money that has been used towards newer real estate developments in the UAE.
Their company is based in Ras Al Khaimah and it is a financial consultancy that they use for their personal investments as well as corporate investments.

They are well aware that financial independence is more important than flashy social status, so they have a Nissan Juke instead of going around in a Rolls Royce.

Financial independence plays an important role in well-being. Financial independent people are usually happier than those who are not.

If you are able to continue your same lifestyle now when you retire, and you are able to survive future financial crisis, then you are financially independent.

Financial independents people are clear about future goals and being clear about their goals make them able to budget accordingly and calculate future expenses too.

How you should invest? Medical care for yourself and your family is much as important as investing in assets and corporate tax-free structures. Buying products or services that improve your business can only benefit you in the long run, such as courses on financial managements or more efficient technologies for your business.

Remember that your funds look better in a secure tax-free investment accounts rather than on your body with luxury dresses or in your toys through expensive toys.

Some Personal Finance Best Practices

I noticed some habits that are very useful to generate the necessary means to start a successful investment career,

Think of money not as a way to buy happiness, but as a way to buy a special kit that protects your wealth from worries, crises, dangers. And this ultimately leads to an happier life.

It can't buy you directly peace or emotions, but it can buy you the comfort and security for yourself and your family and can support your future ambitions.

Some people set goals too high, and often they get demotivated halfway through it so it is important to start the right way.

1. **Don't set unachievable goals, or too-high goals, set "medium" goals.**

Social media today is constantly pushing things to extremes.

Pininterest and Instagram posts constantly tell us through their posts that to be successful and rich you need to live in that tropical resort, or you need to drive that expensive Lamborghini.

The reality is that for most of us, that simply isn't applicable.

Maybe the Harvard graduate trust-funder has enough cash in the bank, right knowledge and powerful connections to dream big and launch a start-up. For the single mom holding two simple jobs and paying also student's loans, things look a little different.

So, there's no shame, and a lot of sense, in being realist and set your goals in the right way by not aiming too high. Remember, we want to protect our wealth and create the financial resources to support our dream lifestyle that doesn't automatically coincide to what the social media wants to imprint in our minds.

Think for yourself and do not let other people think for you.

This means taking accurate decisions in what to take risk in, and in some other topics there is no shame in wanting to play it safe and protect yourself.

When you do decide to take a risk, that can be a new business, a new investment or a new career in a new city, be open to calculate the financial risk, opportunity-cost and logistics.

2. Be open about financial resources

It's odd, but even in today's era of constant communication, people simply don't like to talk about money.

People, it seems, are more comfortable talking about intimate matters than their own salaries.

But just like your "intimate matters" probably won't improve if you never talk about it, neither will your attitude to money.

When you feel free to talk about money, with your financial advisor or with you partner for example, you will notice that also the quality of your lifestyle will improve.

You will notice that you will become more confident with your own finances.

Money helps you to support the dream lifestyle you aim at, this mean that you should not be obsessed about it but should look at it in a fun and relaxed way.

This also mean that you should be open to ways of producing money, of investing and obviously to protect the financial resources you hard earned.

Now I will go through some financial management best practices that are also slightly touched on our website www.plutusfinancialprotection.com

Have a track of all your expenses through mobile apps

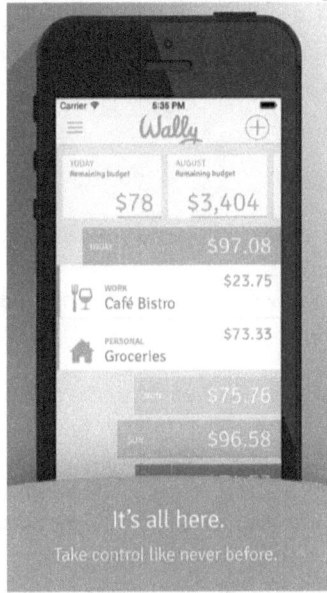

Take advantage of technology. Now there are simple mobile apps that help you track all your expenses.

You can start by seeing where you spend the most and where you can cut some unnecessary expenses without lowering your lifestyle. The app I personally prefer is called Money + and is available for both Android and IOS. You can also opt for Wally, which is shown in the image above.

And don't spend money on credit if you can't pay it off within a month. Sure, credit cards have their benefits – they can help build a credit score and get you air miles. But if you have one, treat it like a debit card.

The day you spend money you can't pay back in a month is the day you sabotage your financial health, because that's when the interest starts to accrue.

Also, don't fall into the CEO lifestyle. We all convince ourselves that we need certain things to live the lifestyle we want, whether that means an iced latte every day, or a taxi home instead of the metro. The reality is that we don't need these things, so we should get over them. The founder of IKEA moves in Sweden with the Bus.

You need to modulate your spending according to your resources, not to the lifestyle you want to portray.

Careful also don't go a week without checking your bank balance at least twice. Just like a reluctant dieter avoids looking at the caloric content of the cake they are devouring, lots of people in poor financial situations just can't bring themselves to look at their account balance.

Learn from Italian grandmothers and cook great food for less.

If you want to reduce eating-out expenses, maybe you can try to learn from them.

The typical Italian grandmother is always cooking something delicious, not based on what she's just seen on Internet but based on what ingredients are in season, which tools she has and what is the occasion.
Grandmother cooks in large quantities, freezes what she can and is focused on everything in moderation rather than any superfood or diet food or that healthy avocados that the social media influencer on Instagram is so eagerly sponsoring.
She wants you to believe she achieved that wonderful look through avocados and chia seeds, but she is not showing you all the session under the plastic surgeon.

So how can you achieve that Italian grandmother status?

The most important thing is to stock your kitchen properly. Whole foods, protein choices like fish, chicken or beef; low glycemic carbs such as pasta or brown rice.
If you've got good olive oil, some salt and pepper, dried chilis, spices, herbs, garlic and onions at home you can already make something delicious and healthy.

Being able to throw something together is a great life skill that will not only enable you to eat well, all the time; it also means fewer costly trips to the grocery store for a specific set of ingredients and less eating-out expenses.

Making a budget is extremely important for planning your spending, saving and investing

All kids wait to be adult and fantasize about it, due to the freedom that this brings. Stay up late, eat what you want, go out and spend the money the way you prefer.

This freedom might be addictive and having a budget might feel restrictive.

But without one, you will be forever financially lost.
So, the first, most important step in your financial diet is to establish what money is coming in and going out. There are lots of useful apps you can use to do this, like Mint or You Need a Budget, but you can also just make a simple spreadsheet.

Whatever you choose, start by entering all your income after tax, like your salary or freelance earnings. Next, enter all of your expenditures. Do this for at least the last two months, and do it honestly, including all expenses – everything from your rent check to that coffee you just bought before starting to read this book.

Once you have done this, you can start to analyze your own expenditure and see where they are more concentrated. The coffee from Starbucks that you consume every day is it really worth 1,100 EUR per year?

Simply analyzing your budget should lead you to some sensible conclusions about your financial behavior. But it can also be helpful to introduce a system to guide your future behavior.

The 50/20/30 plan is a simple way to ensure that your spending is under control and your savings are at a sensible level. Here, 50 percent of your income should go on fixed costs, like your rent and utilities. Twenty percent should go to lifestyle or variable costs, like your dining out, groceries and clothing. And finally, 30 percent should be saved and invested.

This system works well because it gives an easy-to-understand framework against which to judge your expenditures. If you see that you are spending 40 percent of your income on lifestyle expenditures, and only saving 10 percent, you know you need to make a few adjustments.
If you do not have a fixed income every month like me, you can calculate this formula on your average monthly income calculated over last year income. And if your income increases, you should try to dedicate your extra income as much as possible to investments and not to increase your fixed and variable costs immediately.

Everyone's breakdown will be a little different – some might only spend 40 percent on their fixed costs, for instance – but the crucial step is coming to grips with the basics: how much money is coming in and what it's being spent on. Only then can you start to think about getting more value out of the money you have.

Save at least 30% of your monthly income

Might seem a bit high but if you plan to retire young and stop working for money having a 30% monthly "investing" power might really make the difference as we mentioned already in the previous paragraph.

Savings do not magically appear. When young, it's easy to think of your current self and your future self as two completely different people and pass the responsibility for saving into "future me".

Many people think that it is enough staying out of debt to protect future finances, so you do not need to save much. But the fact of the matter is, there is only one you and you need to start saving, even if it is just a little, right now.

Saving is not an easy task, but you can trick your mind to help you do it. Imagine that you are adding these investments to your financial freedom fund. If 30% seems impossible to save because you have urgent and important expenses, a 10% is achievable from everyone.

If you ask successful people ways to increase someone's wealth, they will probably answer by telling you that you need a disciplined investment plan.

Choosing the right investment is also not the only way to protect your wealth.
You need discipline in your spending as we mentioned in the previous paragraph, you could also take advantage of some credit card offers but make sure you don't fall into the trap of spending for the points and you do not take advance cash.

If you really want your money to work for you, you'll have to start investing in some stocks or options I.E invest in some paper assets.

This simply means that you become a partial owner of a business, as you own a stake in it. This includes either shares in a public stock market either shares in private equities. Having stocks from a listed stock market has the added benefit of being able to sell them quite quickly as they have high liquidity.

Stocks and options have relatively high return if treated the right way, and if you do not have experience please make sure you follow right people advices or take courses in stock market investments yourself.

Reserve another 10% of your extra income for "emotional spending"

You want to go to that spa, and you don't know if it is a right expense? you want that leather jacket, but you always believed is pricey? Well, why not taking the needed funds from your "ES Account"? Let's have some fun.

The thing is, there is no secret to financial success – it's nothing more than developing a good set of habits. You just have to learn and implement those habits.

Luxuries might be seen only as needless luxuries but ultimately, they impact our quality of life and sometimes we might feel the need to give ourselves a little treat.
Yes, there is no need of a branded belt compared to a normal one, yes there is no need to a designer's couch compared to a standard one but what about giving ourselves some experiences that we will remember?

Remember that what we remember the most are not the things we buy but the experiences that lead into nice memories.

These are valid reasons to cultivate an Emotional Spending fund.

You can take from this fund the money for a spa, for a shooting course or anything that makes you have fun and relax. A relaxed mind is a healthy mind and only through a healthy mind you can achieve important financial goals. You can also take money from this fund to enjoy the treatment of a famous 5-star restaurant. Remember; you are creating memories, and you are just using extra money for it so you should not feel guilty either.

Relocate your small business in a better fiscal jurisdiction

Do you know that relocating your business does not mean necessary moving everything or expanding abroad? With a simple new free zone or offshore company, you can start an activity abroad and benefit of the fiscal treatment in that region.

You can open a branch of your small company or an entire new company in UAE easily and remotely.

We will go in detail of these procedure in the next chapters.

Prepare a financial safety net in case of unemployment or loss of income

Financial worries can be responsible for keeping us up at night. Being taxed in our mind as well as on our financials is detrimental to our health. How to keep financial worries away? You might want to start to prepare an emergency fund, something like a risk reserve that corporations allocate for their earnings.

Ideally, you should have enough in an emergency fund to cover three to six months of average living expenses. You can finance this fund through your savings at the beginning, once is ready.
This money should be not easily accessible to you, you can put it in an offshore account or in a different bank's savings account.

The main reason for having a fund such as this is so that you have something to fall back in the case business does not go as expected or in case you lose your job as employee.

So, you should not take money from this account if your fridge stops working or your car breaks down. This fund is only for financial emergencies, to cover your most basic living expenses in case of loss of regular income.

Losing your job or losing your major source of income means that you'll need something to see you through while you look for new employment or explore new opportunities.

You also need to bear in mind that, if your line of work is quite specialized, you're going to need longer to find a job that fits your specific skill set; simply put, an executive is going to need more time for the job hunt than a waiter.

That means you're going to need a larger emergency fund to see you through. Thankfully, it's not that complicated to create an emergency fund. You just need to follow a few basic rules.

First off, look at your monthly living costs and work out how big you'll need your emergency fund to be. By now you should be familiar with expense tracking apps and you should know where you spend the majority of your money.

Then, apply for a high-yield savings account. CBI Bank in United Arab Emirates has an excellent e-saver account that gives almost net 3% per year which is above inflation.

Afterwards, to combat your bad habits, you might want to install an automatic payment to this emergency fund account directly from your current account. This until you cover six months of living expenses.

This method is the easiest way to get your emergency fund growing and ensures that you won't be spending your liquid assets on too many luxuries like movie tickets or fancy dinners.

The other thing to consider is which expenses you should immediately cut out if you hit hard times.

Cutting out restaurants is an obvious solution, but you might even need to consider moving to a cheaper apartment if financial issues seem likely to go on for a while. Remember that food, water and shelter are the only things we need to survive. Comfort might be secondary.

Usually, when people get to thinking about money, their thoughts head to the next big thing.

That could be putting a down-payment on a house, buying a car or setting up a college fund for the kids. But your first financial priority should actually be about what comes last. When and if you hit hard times remember that you will not be seen as attractive as before in the market and many people will abandon you easily.
That is also a great period to see if your so thought effective network is really that effective and your so named best friends are really your best friends.

When you shine you are surrounded by people that want a piece of your success but when you fail all these people will disappear quickly and that is when you will see also the true value of your network. Having a well-structured emergency fund keeps your life expenditures going, the most impellent stresses are covered, so you can focus on rebuild your strength as nobody else will do that for you.

Do not fall into the trap of immediately increasing your lifestyle expenses once you get a pay raise or new income from new businesses or better dividends from existing investments.

At the end of your professional life comes retirement.

The reason for that is plain: retirement isn't optional – not like buying a house! Almost everyone is going to retire, and the gap between retirement and death can be very many years indeed. Your mental and physical energies eventually are going to deteriorate, so your income producing power is going to decrease as well.

Having solid assets, strong financial structures with minimized taxation can only help you achieve a more fulfilling retirement. You should start thinking long term as soon as possible to avoid getting stressed in a later period in your life where you have less energies.

If you wait too long, you'll need to put aside an awful lot towards your retirement fund for it to function as it should. If you wait as long as your late thirties or early forties, we're talking around 40 percent of your monthly earnings.
And that's a lot of financial stress.
It doesn't matter if you have student debt, and it makes no difference if you want to save money for a property investment – what comes first should be your retirement plan that can coincide with your investment plan. Starting early might be the key to ensure a comfortable retirement.
Do not fall into the trap of thinking about now only, you do not need to renounce to much at the end to ensure you have a sustainable retirement. Many pension funds successfully provide to that, and a monthly deposit to them might be an easy and effective idea.

And investing for retirement is not different than investing in general, while many financial planners suggest to invest in bonds, mutual funds and monetary funds for your retirement; I remain with the suggestion that investments with low risk are quit pointless while a portfolio mix of medium and high risk investment might be a superior choice.

But of course, saving and investing for your retirement is only one part of the equation. You have to work out what you'll actually do during that time.

It might sound great to be a retiree who goes to the beach or lounges in the sun. But after only a few weeks, that kind of life might become boring.
It can even lead to depression.

So, while you are young, take some time to explore your hobbies and learn skills that can be used in retirement as well. You can use vacations or mini-retirement period to learn those skills.

Ideally, these should be activities that you lose yourself in, where time just flows.

So, for, example, if you think playing an instrument might be what you need in retirement, you should start practicing now. If you like seafood and enjoy fishing, you should cultivate these skills now.

By the time you retire, you'll be proficient enough to enjoy it fully. It will feel like a constructive use of your time and, more than this, you'll have less chance of getting frustrated by learning an entirely new skill at an advanced age.
Learning a skill that can be used also when your physical capacities deteriorate might be a very wise choice.

So now you've got the lowdown. You now know how to increase your financial happiness, how to plan ahead and how to put aside what you need for your savings. Whether it's an emergency fund or planning for major expenses, you know how to approach the challenge and keep yourself financially happy.

Do not invest in what you don't know

Do not follow the friend's tip, or the investment done from everyone else. Alternative investments usually are the highest on ROI but do not invest in anything you have zero

knowledge about. You have 2 choices: you either study the investment properly or you can follow the advice of someone who has done that investment and got proven results.
All these best practices are pretty much necessary to ensure you start protecting your finances.
Afterwards, you might consider of getting a residence or a citizenship in a place that will limit or eliminate your taxation exposure.

By setting up a company in United Arab Emirates for example and getting your own residence visa you will also eliminate any taxation on your personal level.

And if you register also at your own country's consulate as a foreign residence, you will even be able to transfer your funds to your home country with a simple wire transfer.

Be consistent in your investments, to allow your money to grow even when you are sleeping

It's hard to be patient. Who isn't tempted by short-term rewards?
But what long-term investment options can you really trust?

Here's how you take full advantage of these. Let's assume that you have minimal or null knowledge of the investment world. You might want to start with investing in a mutual fund of investments. These organizations take a commission from your money should your investment being profitable.
BlackRock, Templeton, Carmignac are some famous funds management companies.

You can open an investment account after having a minimized taxation personal and company structure, then you want to look for mutual funds whom capitalize their returns. Sticking to the well-known brands like Templeton or BlackRock is not a bad idea, especially if you are new in the investment world.

Then, stay true to the plans that you've created to lead you to an improved life and add the magic ingredient – time. It won't happen overnight, but slowly, steadily, you too will achieve good returns.

Ask yourself a question: are you working for your money, or is your money working for you? If you are stuck thinking about working for your money, it's time to become your money's boss.

Make it work for you, as soon and as much as possible, by investing it.

Whether you are able to put away a dollar a day or ten, you should start doing so as soon as you can.

Being young is a secret shortcut to increasing your wealth, because it means that your money has more time to multiply.

To understand how this happens, you need the rule of 72.

The rule of 72 shows how long it will take any investment to double in value. You just need to divide the number 72 by the annual interest rate, or return, you'll receive on any investment or savings account. That gives you the number of years until your original money is doubled. For example, investments with a return of 7 percent will double your money in 10.28 years. So, invest EUR 1,000 in a fund returning 7 percent a year, and in a decade, you'll have EUR 2,000, without you needing to do any work for it.

Now that you understand how your money can work for you, you realize that a dollar saved and invested is not the same as a dollar spent.

Let's say you are thinking about spending 100 EUR on a new dress. The dress is nice, but you can now see that your choice is not between spending the 100 EUR or saving 100 EUR; it's between spending 100 EUR now, or having 200 EUR in ten years' time, 400 EUR in 20 years' time and 800 EUR in 30 years' time.

So, if you think investing is something that only old people do, don't be fooled. Being young gives you an advantage when it comes to investing: the sooner you start, the more time your money has to multiply.

Investing is probably easier than you think

For many of us, thinking about investing conjures up images of men on a trading floor, shouting into telephones as they buy and sell stocks and bonds.

The good news is that the reality of investing is very different and much simpler than that. But before diving in, there are two things you need to do.

The best starting point is probably a pension funds account, although I suggest learning the investment world yourself and start to invest your own money by yourself pretty quickly.

You can, for example, invest in low-risk funds like index funds, which track overall performance of an index like the New York Stock Exchange's Dow Jones. Or, if you feel confident enough, you could start to pick individual stocks to buy.
Then when you become a little bit more expert, you can start to take a look at other options. Investing in the stock market first and before other types of investment is helpful to make yourself familiar in the investment world, in low risk and higher liquidity options.

Before you know it, you'll be a full-fledged investor who can sit back and relax, happy in the knowledge that your money is working for you.
Starting with stock market investments will give you the necessary confident to start other types of investments as well.

The Emotional Impacts on Wealth

Fear and Greed can drive financially ignorant people to make irrational decisions.

When it comes to money, everyone experiences two basic emotions: greed and fear. If you have money, you are likely to focus on all the new things it can buy (greed). If you don't have it, you worry you might never have enough (fear).

People who are ignorant about how to manage their finances are especially prone to letting these emotions drive their decision-making. What distinguishes us from animals is our ability to make rational decisions and not emotional decisions. So do not be an animal, be an human, and do not make emotional decisions.

For example, let's say you received a promotion and a salary raise.

You could invest the extra money into something like stocks (paper assets) or alternative investment, which would earn you money over time or you could gratify yourself with a new toy such as a car or a house.

If you are a financially ignorant person who's not protecting his/her wealth, this is where you become a victim of your emotions.

The fear of losing money prevents you from investing in stocks or other assets because of the perceived risks and because the friend of the friend of your friend lost money investing, even though such investments would bring you wealth in the long-term.

At the same time, greed inspires you to spend your increased salary on a better lifestyle, for example by buying a bigger house, which will make your banker very happy due to the mortgage you will subscribe for it.

That's it, by now you should know that this will make you still stuck in the E category with one line of income and also in highest tax-paying quadrant.

By building up your financial knowledge about investments, risk, debt, taxation and with consultation with qualified professionals you will be in a better position to make rational decisions – even in the face of greed and fear.

Fear and greed can drive financially ignorant people to make irrational decisions that ultimately attack their wealth.

You can start the journey toward personal wealth development & protection at any point in your life, but the earlier is the better.

Regardless of age, the best way to get started is by appraising your finances, setting yourself goals, acquire the education necessary to reach them and relocate whenever possible your wealth in fiscal jurisdictions that protects you.

To protect your wealth, you must learn to take risks.

Insanity is defined as doing the same thing over and over again and expecting different results. By this logic, if you're looking to change your current financial state, you'll need to start handling your finances differently.

The biggest change you most likely need to make is learning to take risks. All financially successful people have taken risks to get where they are, and they are successful because they manage rather than fear these risks.

Taking risks means not always being balanced and safe with your money, which is what you're doing when you put it in basic checking and savings accounts at the bank.

Instead of playing it safe, try investing your money in an alternative investment in a fiscal paradise. This has the change of generating much more wealth in a short period of time and give you also the opportunity of obtaining a new residence and sometimes even a new citizenship for increased mobility and improved taxation affection.

Diversification and investment are the best protections against bad times. Taking risks means reducing risks.

You can think of the economy as acting like a hydraulic system: when something goes down, something else goes up. Therefore, you have chances to even use crisis at your advantage, like I did in 2009 when I started investing in the stock market.
Diversification can be done in many different ways: Industry wise and geographic wise are the most common.

Wealthy people don't become wealthy by taking foolish risks though.

When you think of a wealthy person, you may think of a flashy Wall Street trader making audacious deals that turn her into a millionaire overnight.
Reality is that in the investment world it is fundamental to diversify

The idea that wealthy people make always very risky investments is just a myth.

For example, not one of the millionaires in my studies mentioned investing in single stock only and it's clear to see why – the risk is just too great.

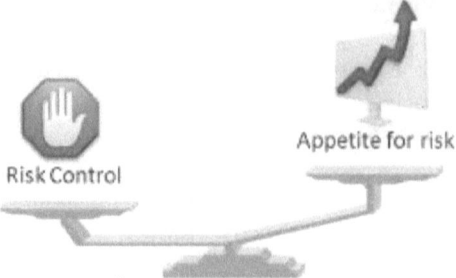

Risk Management strategy

When you buy a single stock, you're putting all of your eggs in one basket. If that stock fails, you can say bye bye to your hard-earned money.
A portfolio that includes businesses in different geographies, alternative investments, real estate, mutual funds, 5-6 types of stocks listed in the stock market might be a superior choice.

Then there are cryptocurrencies. Bitcoin, Ethereum, Qash and the like get a lot of press they days.

They're hot, new and they have the potential to make people wildly rich. But cryptocurrencies are literally made-up currency. They're untested, completely unregulated and no one is accountable for them.

Yes, there are people that make their money with cryptocurrencies, but chances that you will replicate them are quite small and they are extremely unpredictable and not backed up from any real asset yet. It is certainly worth to study them a bit and to know how they are created as in future they *might* change the way we perceive money entirely but this is beyond the purpose of this book and myself I need more experience and practice before I can talk about them.

What about the other end of the spectrum? Well, there are low-risk investments like certificates of deposit and bonds. They're generally very safe bets, but they also tend to be pretty low reward as a result. Many rich people don't buy these – they avoid both the high- and low-risk extremes. In fact, 79 percent of millionaires say that their paths to wealth was very predictable – a medium risk investment portfolio. And what did they invest in most often through those plans? Growth stock mutual funds, which balance a reasonable, diversified risk with a good potential for growth.

The truth is: statistically wealth is not generated from high or low risk investments. Most of wealth is generated by moderate portfolio. That is: *investing is like everything else in life, it has to be done in moderation.*

Tax Havens

Although this book is not encouraging to "hide" your funds in tax havens and is not encouraging to evade taxation, I think that is important to know some story behind it. Keep in mind that our objective is to show you how you can optimize your taxation and how you can protect yourself from excessive taxation.

The first tax havens appeared after World War I, and their numbers grew as the time went on.
As you can imagine, world wars are expensive. And after World War I, many European nations raised income taxes in an effort to rebuild communities and assist veterans.

An extreme case is post-war France. In 1924, he country's previous top-tier income tax (2%) had been raised to a staggering 72%.

Similar tax increases were popping up across the continent, and, as a result, wealthy Europeans devised methods for dodging these taxes – most commonly, by moving their money to other countries.

Switzerland was the most obvious tax haven. A neutral state during World War I, Switzerland was untouched by combat and had no reason to raise taxes, and it also had a well-established banking network with high interest rates.

By 1938, Swiss banks stored ten times more foreign wealth than in 1920. At the time, this amount accounted for 2.5% of the total wealth of European households and would equal about 130 US Billion in today's value.

Understand the tax code to help you minimize your taxes.

Taxes detract a lot of personal wealth, but I'm shocked to notice how most people don't bother to find out how they can minimize the taxes they pay. Evading taxes is different than minimizing taxes. Sometimes I even get the reply "I don't have free time to look for it". The reality is that all time is free, it is up to us how we want to allocate it and we should not let external circumstances to dictate how our time is spent.
The media and the government and the schools do not want you to know how you can minimize your fiscal impact, so you should interest in that yourself!

There are many ways to achieve tax minimization.

One way to reduce taxation is to invest your money through the coverage of a nice Free Zone company located in the UAE. If you invest through your company, the money you make from your online stock account for example, is not taxed anymore

When you are an employee, you earn, get taxed, and then try to live on what's left. When you are protected by a company - assuming is not located in the UAE - you earn, invest or spend as much as you can, and then get taxed on what's left (if any taxation applicable).

People are always reluctant to pay taxes especially if too high and so should you. If you do not want to relocate to another country you can still open a side business tax-free abroad, and the next chapters will show you how.

Balance work and life – your real wealth is your free time.

Remember that money is just an instrument to achieve your dream lifestyle, not a goal.
If growing your business means depriving yourself of more time, then you are actually decreasing your wealth instead of protecting it.
How to achieve the balance between work and play that allows for a more balanced and rich life?
I will repeat once again, exactly like "all time is free" and there is no duty time and free time distinction, there is also no strict division between your professional and private life. There is only one life: your life and there is only one time: your time.

Consequently, you should eliminate arbitrary time boundaries, and instead do things when "the spirit moves you". If you want to complete some work on Saturday night, and then go lay on the beach on Monday morning, that is fine: go for it. You are the master of your own time so use it as you wish and do not let the society dictate your life.

Secondly, the secret to a fulfilling life lies in variety. As Nietzsche once wrote "a day has a hundred pockets if you know what to put in them" so you should make an earnest effort to never stop learning and to push yourself to try new things and new experiences.

CHAPTER SUMMARY

SECRET 1:
Protecting your wealth starts from good spending habits

SECRET 2:
Tracking your income and expenses is important for protection and development of your wealth

SECRET 3:
There are many legal ways to protect your income and patrimony for taxation, and there is nothing wrong in pursuing them

SECRET 4:
Balance work and life, money is not a goal but an instrument to achieve your dream lifestyle

CHAPTER 5
DETAX YOUR TIME

Your time is one of the most valuable assets you have, because it is limited and shrinking by the second. So why not use science to ensure you make the most of it?

Ultimately, finding more happiness and success starts with choosing better experiences to spend your time with.

It's pretty common for concerns about free time to take a back seat to concerns about being more productive.

Indeed, if you were raised in a capitalist society, you may think that time not spent earning money is time wasted. I will go against this belief, our time should not be devoted solely to produce financial resources but should be equally dedicated to make money, protect wealth and enjoy life.

Our desire to be efficient also explains why we tend to feel like we have less free time than we actually do.

There are also reasons of why we feel we do not have free time.
At the top of this list is the fact that people spend a daily average of three and a half hours interacting with their phones.

This often comes from the fact that with so many emails, texts and social media updates arriving daily, there's an anxiety-inducing fear of missing out on something – known as FOMO – which results in hours spent just keeping up with your digital life.

There is also another factor that comes into play which plays with our psyche: it is called the law of intermittent rewards addiction. This applies to any social media like that you receive, any new follower on Instagram, any achievement on your smart phone game... the reward triggers your brain to produce dopamine, and the pleasant feeling makes you continue seeking for that virtual reward.

Many businesses are starting to prohibit the usage of mobile phones in their restaurants or clubs, to encourage people to interact with each other instead of interacting only with their phones.

In our yacht business, we even created no-smartphones events, where people can enjoy partying on the yacht and socialize with the people available in the middle of the sea... at that time. Sometimes when I see people staring at their phone for the latest WhatsApp message, I confiscate the phone and I tell them "the boat is your WhatsApp, talk with the people around you"

But here's the thing about productivity: even though we place a high value on work and productivity, they aren't the only important things in life, especially when it comes to feeling happy and satisfied.

According to multiple studies from institutions like Harvard Business School and Cornell University, what really brings happiness into people's lives are experiences.
If better life experiences lead to happiness, and happiness is a great precursor of success.

Conventional wisdom usually tells us that happiness is a byproduct of success, and yet a lot of evidence suggests that it's actually the other way around.

What all of this adds up to is that positive experiences lead to happiness, which in turn leads to success. So, to achieve success, we should try to have positive experiences.

For enduring happiness, choose experiences that add to your own heroic story
when considering whether or not an activity is going to be a worthwhile way of spending your time, the first question you can ask yourself is: Will it add to my Story?

Any valuable experience will add to your story by ticking off one or all of the items on the checklist. Water has been always a part of my story, that is why I decided to involve in a business related to the sea.

For example, if you had an eye-opening experience while on a yoga retreat in India, that would count as transformational, intense, extraordinary and significant.

Ultimately, experiences like this inform the kind of people we are, and they also form the narrative of our own life stories.

There are two popular versions of all the heroic stories we find so satisfying. The first is called "The Man in a Hole Story," introduced by the American writer Kurt Vonnegut, Jr.
It suggests that every hero in a narrative starts out in a good place, then gradually sinks into a hole of misfortune before being restored to good fortune by the end of the story.

The other version of this story is what scholar Joseph Campbell calls "The Hero's Journey," which is a more circular tale. It starts out in the ordinary world, where the hero accepts a "call to action" that requires perseverance through many trials and tribulations.

Through this process, the hero learns new skills, overcomes the supreme ordeal, receives a reward and returns home. In the end, he shares the gifts and wisdom he acquired, and in doing so forever changes the ordinary world into a new world.

By placing yourself in the hero's role, you cannot only recognize what your particular call to action is but can also begin to be more adventurous and understand that difficulties and struggles are crucial to our stories and shouldn't be avoided. It is through these challenging experiences that we acquire the tools that allow us to reach our goals and slay our own metaphorical dragons.

Events that provide change and transformation are key to finding fulfillment

Once you place yourself in your own hero's journey, you can start to see that change – Transformation – is the name of the game.

After all, if you were watching a story in which the hero wasn't changing in some way, it would be pretty boring and maybe even sad, right?

Well, the same holds true for your life, and its why change and personal development are key to feeling happier and more fulfilled. Role Playing Games are for the same reason successful because they allow the protagonist and the player of the game to feel that there is a Constant Development with a Learning Curve.

Remember, one of the four basic needs which is "to learn"?

Having problems and solving them releases dopamine, which makes us feel good and fulfilled.
This is a good time to consider two simples but revealing questions: Looking back over the past ten years, how much do you think you've changed, on a scale of one to ten?
Now, how much do you think you'll change over the next ten years?
Have you ever felt that the people around of you have changed after you come back from a long trip or from many years of living abroad?

Guess what, they have not changed. You have changed, therefore your perception of them has changed.

If a *go and become* trip might bring some changes and development in yourself, significant changes are often unplanned.
And remember, we tend to overestimate how much we can achieve in one year, but we greatly underestimate what we can achieve over 5 or 10 years.
Once you understand that change is a key part of a fulfilling life, you can start actively seeking it out, by finding experiences that bring new inspiration, new skills and other transformative elements into your life.

Step out of your comfort zone, start protecting your finances, automate your work, look for a more fulfilling lifestyle.

Let's take vacationing, for instance. There are basically three ways you can approach a vacation: fly and flop, find and seek, or go and become.

With **fly and flop**, personal development is not on the menu. Fly and flop might involve going to a resort and engaging in passive experiences like lying in the sun, eating familiar foods and reading books and magazines that require very little effort on your part.
While it might be relaxing, this approach results in some pretty dull stories to tell others back home.

Find and seek involves more active engagement. You travel to new places with the intent to explore, or maybe attend a music festival like Burning Man or Tomorrowland. You'll see new things and have some interesting stories to tell, but for the most part it's an experience that any other sightseer or concertgoer might have.

The **go and become** approach, however, offers a real chance for transformation.
In this scenario, your vacation would come with a purposeful intent to learn inspirational things about different cultures and customs, or new skills like painting, boating or traditional sushi techniques. It might involve learning new investments or taxation structures to protect your wealth; or it might involve a spiritual retreat of some kind.

Whatever the case may be, it will include very personal, financial and possibly very transformational, experiences – and therefore a great story.

Humans like stories, and personally I always loved to make my own stories. Imagine becoming old and having many stories to tell your grandchildren: wouldn't that be great?

Valuable experience that lead to happiness are more likely to take place in nature and away from the online world.

Let's first consider the benefits of nature.

Around 1990, Japanese researchers began looking into the claims of health benefits surrounding a pastime known as shinrin yoku, or forest bathing – and, sure enough, the claims appeared to be valid.

Compared to walks on a treadmill, these immersive forest walks were far more effective at reducing tension, anger and fatigue, as well as blood pressure and cortisol levels, while at the same time improving mood.

There's also the revealing evidence gleaned from the 20,000 or so users of the Mappiness app, who periodically entered their mood and activity while the app recorded GPS and weather data.

Ultimately, the data showed that people were unhappiest while at work, sick in bed, or commuting to work, and that they were happiest while in nature – especially when close to water. Happiness levels in coastal areas were generally six points higher than in urban areas for example.

There's a biological factor at work here. Scientists believe we're simply predisposed, from an evolutionary perspective, to enjoy the calming sights, sounds and smells of nature and water. Biological factors also help explain why we should choose to spend more time offline.

Researchers have long known that humans are susceptible to conditioning. You may be familiar with the psychologist Ivan Pavlov, who over a century ago conditioned dogs to salivate with hunger – not in the presence of food, but at the sound of a metronome that signified the arrival of food.

Interaction with your smartphone is much like gambling on a slot machine: what's at work is a system of operational conditioning known as **intermittent variable rewards**.

This means you're interacting with a system that offers an inconsistent promise of large or small rewards. And when this happens, even the most intelligent people can end up picking up their phones 300 times a day, checking how many likes their latest Instagram or Facebook post has been liked, or for the latest text message.

The problem is that, as multiple studies in the US and Europe show, too much time online leads to feelings of isolation, stress, depression and insomnia.
Fortunately, however, if you start spending less time online now, your mood and your productivity can improve immediately.
Engage in activities that connect you with others to avoid potentially fatal effects on loneliness,
While solitude and some time alone can be a nice change of pace from time to time, no one enjoys feeling lonely. I personally prefer solitude only when I'm writing, or I am reading.

This might sound obvious enough, but what you may not know is just how dangerous loneliness can be.

Over time, persistent loneliness has been proven to cause stress and create more protein fibrinogens in your body, which clog arteries, increase blood pressure and make you more likely to get diabetes and have a heart attack.

What's more, in compiling seven years' worth of data from nearly three and a half million people, researchers found that loneliness increased a person's chances of death by 29 percent. Meanwhile, social isolation increased that chance by 26 percent, and living alone by 32 percent.
Remarkably, these statistics show that loneliness is deadlier than type 2 diabetes or smoking 15 cigarettes a day.

Relationships. Curbing loneliness is about finding ways to connect with other people. And the good news is that there are many ways of doing this.

Remember the chapter on personal network? Having productive relationships might not only make you a happier and more productive person but might help your career advance and your business become more successful.

Basically, the way to be less lonely is to do something interesting – anything, really. Most experiences involve other people in some way, whether you're outside playing sports or indoors playing a board game.

But even if you're pursuing solitary experiences like meditating, reading an interesting book or working on a painting, psychologists have found that these activities can still provide a sense of belonging in the larger sense.

And remember, whenever you have an interesting experience, it gives you a good story to tell, and sharing stories is one of the best ways to form bonds with others.

Ideally, your experiences speak to who you are as an individual, so think about what you like to do, and then see whether there's a group in your community or online that you can join. If you like to go hiking, there are plenty of outdoor groups; if you like to read, join a book club, or start your own.

Check out what's going on in your community. It's highly likely that there's a group or association doing something that you find interesting. If not, there may be a festival within a reasonable distance that you can attend. Networking events are great, if you live abroad a starting point might be to be a member of the business council of your own country in that specific country you are residing now. Nowadays we have internet to help us join communities, and my favorite platform has always been meetup.com. I use myself this platform to organize networking events on the yachts around specific topics. You can group easily people that are interested in the same topic and guess what: people that come from this platform will really interact with other people present at the event and not stare at their smartphone all night.

Personality & Time Management

What distinguishes humans from animals is that animals are slaves to external stimuli and can only react to these stimuli in the preprogrammed way that is in their nature.

We humans, in contrast, irrespectively of which personality and values and beliefs that we have, can reflect on a stimulus before responding to it, and we can even reprogram ourselves to respond in a specific, desirable way.

This means that instead of just reacting to the world around us, we have the ability to proactively influence it.

But even though we all have this capacity for proactivity, many people still choose to be reactive and allow external circumstances to dictate their behavior and emotions, exactly like they allow someone else to take control over their own finance them and TAX them. Phrases like "it was not my fault" or "it's out of my hands" unfortunately are extremely common.

People who are proactive make their own destiny and influence others. They assume responsibility for their own lives and make conscious choices about their behavior.

Consider Viktor Francis, who, during World War II, was imprisoned in multiple German concentration camps. In the midst of this misery, he decided that, although his guards controlled everything about his environment, he was still free to choose how he responded to his circumstances. Though suffering terribly, he could imagine himself in future, happier days, teaching his students what he had learned in the camp. His freedom existed in the small gap between the outside stimuli he faced and his response to it. No one could take away this last freedom, and he nurtured it until, like a tiny spark that blazes into a roaring fire, it inspired those around him, including some of the guards.

Similarly, you too have the power to decide what happens in the gap between a stimulus and your response. Thus, you can change your behavior and your emotions.

Inner character is the driver of true success, and it can be developed.
And remember, every personality needs a purpose.
Whether it's writing novels or raising a family or becoming a millionaire, a purpose give meaning to life, and you get a sense of direction and duty as well. And yet very few people define their purpose, which should be aligned with your personality, values and beliefs.

Purpose is crucial because, without it, you won't know how to contribute to the world, and contribution is the second lever of success. To identify your purpose, start by asking yourself 3 questions:

- What is my society lacking?
- What am I good at?
- How can I contribute leveraging my skills and my personality?

Keep in mind that your purpose might be right in front of your eyes. Combining yourself with the environment around you might be the key. And if it does not work you either change yourself or you change environment.

For example, consider the protagonist of the film Mr. Holland's Opus. He dreams of becoming a brilliant composer, but he's forced to work as a music cheater, a job that he initially dislikes. But the years go by and he begins to love his students. In the end, he does not become a famous composer. Instead, he pours his passion into teaching and contributes by helping thousands of students.
So, remain open to the possibility that, without realizing it, you may have already found your purpose – all you have to do is identify it.
Once you have figured out how to contribute to the society, you can start creating your tax-free structures that enable you to prioritize and act accordingly.

Prioritizing is a matter of differentiating urgent task but not important with important but not urgent and urgent but not important.

Time Management Matrix

Stephen R. Covey popularized the Eisenhower's Time Management Matrix in his book The 7 Habits of Highly Effective People, stating that we live a fourth generation of time management, more effective, in which managing time itself is no longer the aim, but managing where to focus at any particular time is the goal we need to pursue.

	Urgent	Not Urgent
Important	**Quadrant I** • Crisis • Pressing problems • Deadline driven projects	**Quadrant II** • Relationship building • Finding new opportunities • Long-term planning • Preventive activities • Personal growth • Recreation
Not Important	**Quadrant III** • Interruptions • Emails, calls, meetings • Popular activities • Proximate, pressing matters	**Quadrant IV** • Trivia, busy work • Time wasters • Some calls and emails • Pleasant activities

Important and non-urgent tasks are there for your long-term development and should always be prioritized.

Imagine you are a doctor and while performing a heart surgery, a nurse runs asking you to attend a phone call. Obviously, you would not go and attend the call as the task of heart surgery is certainly urgent and important. Importance always trumps urgency, so you would not take the call.

This example demonstrates how a higher purpose – in this case, the purpose of saving the patient's life – naturally leads to prioritization of what's most important.
Modern mobile apps help us organizing and prioritizing tasks. It is time you turn your smartphone into being smart, I personally use for myself and for my businesses the Wunderlist application where you can put deadlines and you can star tasks for importance.

In order to become effective, you need to recognize your decision points as well.

Over the course of each day, you engage in all manner of habitual tasks. Think about how many times in your life you've hopped out of bed, gotten dressed, scanned your emails and attended weekly meetings without a second thought.
In these cases, we often switch off and go into automatic to get through our daily routines.

Rarely do we stop to consider whether our routines make sense. It may be that your daily tasks are causing you to waste a great deal of time and energy without even realizing.

Take Dougie. As a consultant, he was required to write a monthly analysis report. But instead of completing this rather important task, Dougie ended up tending his inbox instead, responding to a dozen emails in a trance-like state. Because sorting through his emails is part of his daily routine, Dougie gave it preference over what should have been his real priority. Like Dougie, many of us let routines get in the way of real productivity. So how can we change? By recognizing our decision points. Decision points are those moments in times when a given task is completed or interrupted. At a decisions point, you have the opportunity to consciously choose what you do next.

Let's look at an example. Say a colleague comes to your desk and asks you to go to lunch with him. As a result, you're interrupted in the middle of drafting a report. You then recognize that you've got a decisions point on your hands. You could either decline his offer and continue your work or take a break and get a bite to eat.
By consciously considering your options here, you'll be better able to make a decision that benefits you and your productivity the most. As you become more aware of these points in time between tasks and make fewer impulsive decisions, you'll be able to become more effective with your time.

Time management and Clear Thinking

We use a massive amount of energy in all our interactions with the world, which fatigues our ability to think clearly. This indicates that our capacity for active thought is limited.

Evidence for this limitation can be found as early as 1898, in a study where subjects were instructed to perform a mental task while putting as much physical pressure as possible on a machine that measures force (a "dynamometer").

The results revealed that, when the subjects were engaged in active thought, their maximum physical force was reduced by up to 50 percent.

Furthermore, as you'd expect, performing more than one conscious process simultaneously is even more taxing. The result is that our performance quickly declines when we try to do several mental tasks at the same time. That is, multitasking is greatly overrated!

For example, one study indicated that the constant distraction of emails and phone calls reduce performance in an IQ test by 10 points, on average. This reduced mental capacity is similar to that we experience after missing a night's sleep.

One explanation for this effect is that such interruptions force the brain to spend too much time in a state of alertness.

So, if we want to maintain a good level of performance, we have to conserve the brain's energy for only the most important tasks.

This can mean prioritizing certain tasks above others. But be aware that prioritizing is itself a task that drains energy, so make sure you prioritize when your mind is alert and fresh.

Another way to conserve energy is to turn tasks into routines, as these can be stored as patterns that won't require you giving your full attention to a task. Your brain might proceed in performing these tasks in automatic, with a greatly reduced effort.
Think about when you learn how to drive, at the beginning your greatly focused, after a while you tend to go in autopilot.

Our attention is very easily distracted, but there are strategies for staying focused

In many ways, advances in modern technology have certainly made our lives easier.
But the convenience they provide also comes at a great cost to our ability to focus: the ubiquity of always-on technologies, like the internet and smartphones, means that we have more potential distractions in our lives than ever before.

Whenever we're distracted, our attention is diverted, and refocusing that attention takes time and effort.
In fact, one study revealed that over two hours of office workers' time is consumed by distractions. Another study showed that we spend around eleven minutes on a task before we're distracted, and don't return to our work until twenty five minutes later.

And it's not only external distractions we have to deal with. There are also many internal distractions: the constant stream of thoughts that surface into consciousness and impair our focus – like wondering whether we paid the gas bill or not.

Moreover, every time we try to resist being distracted, we decrease our ability to do so. This is because self-control is a limited resource.

This was demonstrated by a famous study, where participants were placed in a room, alone, with a bar of chocolate. Some of the participants were instructed to resist eating the chocolate, while others were allowed to eat it.

Afterwards, they were all given a challenging mental task to perform.

Those who had managed to resist eating the chocolate gave up on this mental task much sooner than those who hadn't exercised their self-control, suggesting that self-control can become fatigued simply through being used.

So, how then can we maintain our focus when we're surrounded by potential distractions?

Put simply, you have to prevent those distractions from seizing our attention. One way to do this is to develop the habit of "vetoing" those behaviors that distract us. This requires us to turn off all communication devices whenever we need to do any kind of active thinking. Also, you might want to remove any "distraction attraction" from sight in your place of work including any "distraction food" that might lead to overeat so you can start to avoid having candies, biscuits or snacks in sight. If you are a smoker avoid having cigarettes close to you and so on. Your workplace should be as neat and empty as possible to minimize distraction which would ultimately drain your brain power.

Brain chemicals in action

Which would you watch more intensely: a once-in-a-lifetime solar eclipse that lasts only a minute, or the tree outside your window?

If you're like most people, you focus better when you're faced with a tight deadline, or when you are presented with something new and interesting.

That's because being alert and interested sharpens our focus.

For us to be alert, our brains require exactly the right level of norepinephrine, the chemical that's triggered when we're scared. Fear activates our alertness, and alertness is a crucial part of being focused.

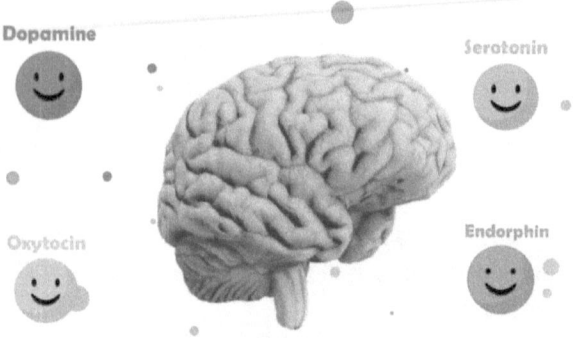

And for our interest to be aroused, our brains need just the right amount of another chemical: dopamine.

Dopamine is triggered whenever we experience something new or unexpected, which means it's an important factor in our becoming interested in something.

However, for our brains to function at their peak, it's crucial that the levels of norepinephrine and dopamine in the brain are not too high and not too low

If these levels are low, our performance will be poor.

Managing your own stress and trying to understand the chemicals that influence your brain might be fundamental for your overall well-being too.

Having a lot of distraction is also mainly responsible for poor performances

By having clear ideas on what to do, and by clearly ranking them in order of urgency and importance you will suddenly see an increase in your performance

This way, you only spend energy on the tasks that really matter.

The timing related to a task to be completed is important as well. Managing smartly deadlines will help you achieve more with less time. This phenomenon is called "Parkinson Law".

Parkinson Law basically states that when we are close to a deadline of a project, we become automatically more productive, minimizing distraction and time wastes and accomplishing more with less.

Managing your deadline and goals is fundamental then to be successful in your field. Remember the application Wunderlist?
Data show that people excellent in time management generally lead a more fulfilling and successful life.

CHAPTER SUMMARY

SECRET 1:
Try to limit your time in the digital world, its mechanism of small rewards might make you addicted to it but ultimately you want to choose to dedicate your time to productive activities or to activities that will add to your own personal story.

SECRET 2:
The **"find and seek"** and the **"go and become"** approach in your holiday planning might lead to interesting stories that will not only add to your own but might be the source of life changing experiences that can even ultimately impact your wealth.

SECRET 3:
Minimize distractions in your workplace. Start to plan your schedule by differentiating what is urgent and important versus what is urgent and not important and not urgent and not important. Prioritizing and delegating tasks is key to time management.

CHAPTER 6
Getting your company license or permit up and running

So, you have already a business and you want to expand it or optimize it.
Or you have an idea and want to start an entire new business.

Or again, you need a corporate structure that can protect your wealth generated abroad and can minimize your own financial taxation.

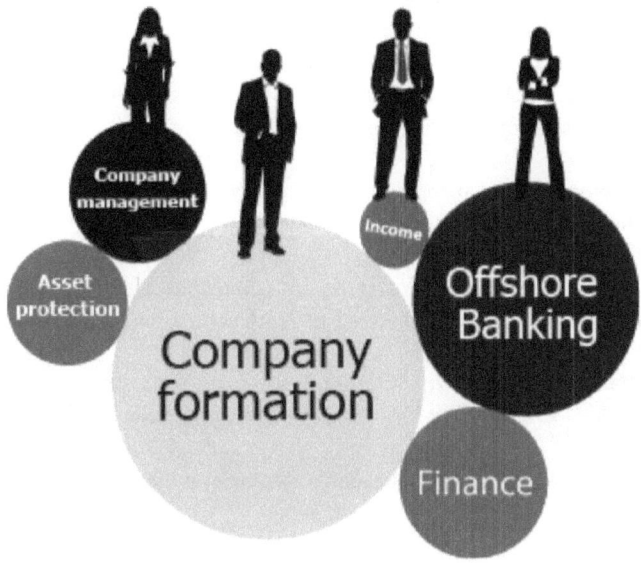

In all these cases, you will need to open a company account abroad who can let you also get another residence with an optimized taxation status.

Starting a new business is exciting, especially if it's one that's closely linked to your skills and passions.

And the best part is, you can launch your dream business without quitting your day job.

It's possible to build a small business in your free time, as long as you do so systematically.

In fact, loads of people who now earn their living from their passion initially built their business in their spare time as a side hustle. And just a single hour a day spent planning over the course of a few weeks is enough to launch a small business.

But, naturally, you need to be careful not to waste your time.

So, don't search out that one big business idea; it's elusive and you don't need it. Instead, answer specific questions:

- What kind of product or service are you going to provide?
- Who are your customers going to be?
- Which of their problems are you going to solve?
- What will your budget look like?
- How can you market your business?
- Which knowledge or skills you will need to run this business?
- What personal connections you might need to develop?

These questions are perfect because you can answer them in detail in your daily hour devoted to your new business.

Then, once you're done planning, you can start spending your daily hour executing your plans, one step at a time – for instance, by advertising your service on a social network.

You'll always be on the safe side if you follow this strategy. You'll be able to rely on the income from your day job and won't have to depend on your new business to succeed.

As a result, you can experiment with your idea, learning a lot in the process while still paying your bills.

And if your business does work out, it will give you a second source of income that will make you even more financially stable. That said, if you really want to quit your 9-to-5 and work on your business full time, you should do it – but only if your business is generating enough money to keep you afloat. That is, you are leaving the E world to enter S and B world in the cashflow quadrants.

You can create your own job description

Plenty of job-finding strategies seem like a good idea initially but prove to be a colossal waste of time.

And, truthfully, most of them are. So, if the well-worn paths don't lead you to career success, just create your own job.

Just try to consider all that time you spent to update your cv, your LinkedIn profile, your cover letters... and it did not work that much right? This because many more people probably more qualified than yourself are using exactly the same method.

This means lots of competitors, so my advice remains networking if you are looking to become an employee... but even better create your own company so you can create your own job description.

Some people even create their own titles. For instance, Tony Bacigalupo nominated himself to be the Mayor of New Work Cities, his coworking space.

You can represent your own work today, by showing to the world the set of skills and expertise that you only have. And remember, everyone has his or her specific set of skills that we acquire during our life.

You do not have to do only one thing!
I personally jumped from stock market investments, to accounting, to tourism and entertainment, to consulting and taxation... these are all fields where I have a passion in and where I am willing to put my time for the cause.

What is your cause?
Are you struggling with the question of what to do with your financial life?
Well, if you are, it might be because you think you need to decide on a single, focused pursuit once and for all.

In reality, you don't need to pick a niche and stick with it for your whole life; instead, you can adapt your career to your changing needs and interests. A starting point as employee and then slowly creating a side optimized-tax system that grows up to be a lucrative business and eventually takes over might be a great and achievable goal.

After all, you never signed a contract saying you'll do the same thing for the rest of your life. And that's a good thing, because life is seasonal – your needs and interests will change as you do. If you're raising a child, you might appreciate the regular schedule and steady income of a 9-to-5 job. But during other phases, you might prefer the nomadic lifestyle of a travel writer.

A happy life is based on the ability to choose, but you also might want to focus on more than one skill over the course of your career. It's not necessarily to the detriment of your career to pursue multiple interests.

There are lots of ways to live a fulfilling life, so find your passions and devote yourself to every one of them. If you are not clear about what your life the most you can consider working part-time in multiple fields before investing money and time in any project.

Have you ever considered what makes you different and unique as a disadvantage? Don't! It is a competitive advantage to be different from the rest!

Today's marketplace is crowded, and people have more options than ever from which to choose. From bars and restaurants to technological gadgets and mobile applications, it's the ones that offer something unique and different that stand out and succeed.
You can either offer something new and different or you can offer something that is already present in the market but with a better value proposition, for example at a lower price and higher quality.

If you are wondering what kind of successful project to work on for the next year, focus on the ones that have that special feature and stand out from the rest.

You can start by individuating your so called "passion" but beware that "passion" is greatly overrated. Yes, it's much easier and more enjoyable to spend time on things we are passionate about. But don't forget that this passion should be marketable and lucrative otherwise you might not reach your financial freedom with it.

It can take a lot of time to master something or perfect a certain skill, so it's wise to turn your attention to something about which you're passionate and at the same time it is also lucrative.

Studies reveal that it takes about 10,000 hours of practice to become pretty much the master of anything, including learning for example a music instrument.
Those hours will go by much more quickly if you love what you are doing.
But to be successful you have to avoid the pitfalls along the way.

One common pitfall is the tendency to give up after a failure or misstep. Don't fall into this one! Instead, pick yourself up and look at a failure as a chance to learn from your mistakes and make improvements. Progression is the key, including trial and error.

Remember that Success looks like an Iceberg.

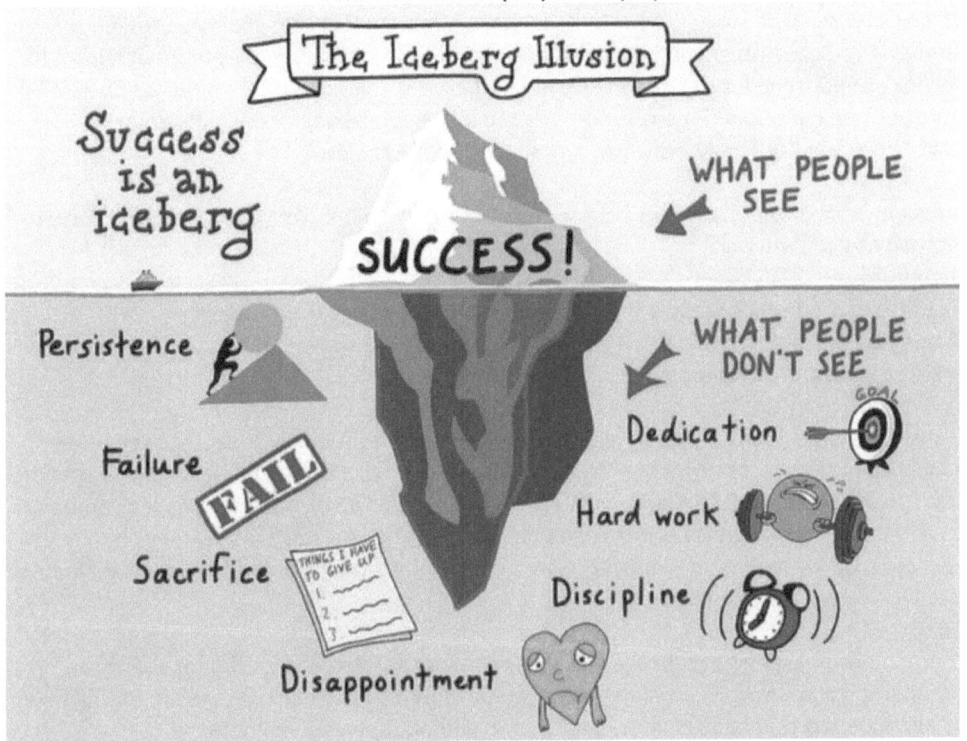

Another pitfall involves being paralyzed by uncertainty about the future. In reality, no one knows what the future holds – even a winning lottery ticket might turn into a future disaster! It's better to focus on the present and creating your opportunities.

Warren Buffet once said, "*stop trying to predict the economy, the market and the elections*".

So, now that you know what to look for – and what to avoid – it's time to follow the plan.

And to have success in business you might think about an alternative strategy too.

When thinking about success in business, many people think big: big companies, big products and big CEOs – like Amazon, Apple, Microsoft.

Thinking about success this way can be really stressful and frustrating. After all, your chances of starting the next industry-conquering giant, creating the next viral product sensation or becoming the next multibillion-dollar start-up founder are pretty low.

But do you really want to be that big? Do you want your life to revolve around making more money, finding new markets and managing large organizations on an ever-increasing scale?

If it is in your scale of values, go for it. If you have a commander personality go for it. Otherwise you can also enjoy the independence of owning your company without having to sacrifice all your time for it. You can also aim to become able to work a limited number of hours per week and spend the rest of them doing what you love, for example enjoying quality time for your family, traveling or pursuing your hobbies.

You might start to think smaller about success, to achieve more. You can take a step back, to take two forward later on.

The ethos of modern capitalism can be summarized in a single word: "more".
On one side of the economic equation, there is the average consumer, who is continually seeking to buy more products and services to consume.

On the other side, there is the average business, which is continually seeking to sell more products and services to grow its profits. The moment it reaches one revenue goal, it sets the target even higher - EUR 1 Million, then EUR 10 Million and so on and so forth. If a company listed in the stock market is performing revenues of EUR 10 Million in 2019, they are already expected to grow their revenues in 2020 by a certain percentage, and if they don't their stock price will immediately go down.

In short, consumers and businesses alike are driven by an insatiable desire for evermore consumption and growth. But there are exceptions. Exactly like most people are paying taxes without having a proper accounting system and without questioning them.

Become the exception.

A new business might have just a simple goal: to ensure enough revenue streams and optimizes costs and taxes in order to secure owners and its employees the necessary amount of comfort, autonomy and free time that they want their lives to have.

For example, Sean D'Souza runs a company called Psychotactics, which provides consultancy services. His growth limit is 300,000 EUR profits per year. Probably he could make more money if he wanted to, but he purposefully chose to restrict his company to this profit goal.

Why not more? Well, sometimes more money brings more problems. Fight with more competitors, secure better suppliers, enter new markets, hire more people.

Generally speaking, more profits require more production, sales and customers, which in turn require more employees, infrastructure and bureaucracy. Expansion might not always be the right choice, as it might even decrease the overall ROI of your company. That means more exhaustion, oversight and work time. Less comfort, less autonomy and less time for other things. And that defeats the purpose of starting a new company to optimize your taxation and to create a side income that might later on become the main one.

If I, myself, start an expansion plan for the Neptune yacht company and I buy more yachts, that would result in time dedicated to hire more employees, another boat to follow in accounting, another boat to supervise in maintenance and ultimately another boat that is taking even hours of bookings from my other boats, ultimately decreasing the overall company ROI even though probably there would be an increase in the overall profits.

For his part, D'Souza would rather be playing with his kids and taking 3 months vacations. If you feel a similar way, then a company of one might be the way for you to go as well.

Single owned companies are different than traditional small businesses or freelancers' forms of employments.
With your own company you can get a United Arab Emirates investor visa as a residence, which lasts three years. It also allows you to open a corporate bank account in UAE, without mentioning your name at all but only the company name.

When starting your company, however, I always suggest it to do it on the side of your job, the same way I did.

From this point on, we are going to examine the process of starting a company of one from beginning to end, step by step. Along the way, we will look at some of the distinguishing features, goals and strategies of a successful company of one.

The first step involves not doing something: don't quit your day job if you have one. Like many single-owned companies, your new business is probably going to grow out of a side gig. It needs to develop into a sustainable enterprise before you can turn it into a company who can supply financial resources to your lifestyle.

Tom Clays worked in marketing for twenty years. In his free time, he pursued a hobby he loved since he was a kid: cartoons. At a party he just did it for fun. Then he started to take side gigs, drawing for clients on weekends and evenings.
He did not quit his job until he built up a solid roster of clients and saved up enough.
That was 2014, since then, with his tax-free company structure, he is making 3 times the money he was making as marketing specialist, while enjoying plenty of time with his family and doing something he loves.

Turn your work into a passion rather than the other way around.
Now that you have resisted the urge to quit your day job and to say bye bye to your boss, what is the first step?

Well, you need to find inspiration first, even if you don't have it already. *Follow your passion.*

There is a problem with that advice though. Unless you happen to be passionate about something that's an in-demand, marketable skill, pursuing your passion is probably not going to be enough to create something that can financially support you.

Sometimes ideas come out of nothing. Myself for example I was celebrating my 24th birthday on a luxury yacht... which gave me the inspiration of starting a yacht charter company myself.

Most people's passions are out of sync with the demands of the market. If you ask any of your friend what is your passion, most probably they will reply about sports, music or art. Yet these fields represent only 3% of all jobs, so it might be impossible for everyone to successfully pursue these passions. And by the way, most people do not even know what their passion is.

This truth is vital to remember. You might have passion for playing football, but you probably won't be the next world champion. The same goes for other passions involving activities that only a tiny percentage of people can earn a living from doing.

You have to be practical. Ask yourself, what is something that you are already good at doing and that other people will pay you to do? If the answer is nothing, what could you get better at doing and make it a marketable skill?

Myself I started this yacht company but yet I was working in a brokerage firm and did not have exactly many connections in the entertainment world or with travel agents and event companies. So, I focused on what I was good at: managing financials.

I managed the cost structure of the company and focused on one specific way to pursue a competitive advantage: offer my clients lower price but higher quality than competitors. And this you can reach it with cost-optimization and accurate financial managements.

Lord Alan Sugar, in United Kingdom, pursued exactly this same competitive strategy for his electronics company Amstrad, to offer higher quality and lower price than competitors.

Then I was fortunate to find partners who had experience in marketing, management and entertainment. If you don't try, you cannot get lucky. You need to create the occasions to let luck come to you.

In other words, don't wait for a financially viable career path to magically materialize from your passion; instead, focus on identifying and developing a marketable skill set now, and allow your passion to emerge from the process of refining, mastering and helping other people with it.

Keep in mind that this is not an easy task, understanding our strengths and skills and how to market them. You might even want to dedicate an holiday for yourself and to understand that, might be a great investment.

Focus on customer service and retention

When you start off on the path of establishing a company, your main competitive edge is just your network, which allows you to be very personable with your clients and to focus on providing them with excellent customer service.

As your company grows, you might be tempted to scale that customization and service. Customer service is crucial to succeeding in today's economy. Customer service not only ensures returning customers but are potent marketing tools as 70% of many businesses are fueled from referrals of existing customers.

Now, whether your goals are to create your next side business, your next activity, or your goal is to simply relocate in a more protected tax-free structure... let's go to the technical and practical side of a business set-up

The Freezone/Offshore Business Setup

Many people prefer starting with classic consulting UAE free-zone license, given its flexibility in terms of opening bank accounts or performing activities but it always depends on the activity you want to start or the activity of your mother company in case you already own a company in your home country.

It is important to have clear ideas on the activity you want to do with this new company as the jurisdiction might change according to your needs.

I strongly suggest making clear ideas and communicate to your consultant what are the exact purposes on this company. It might be a trading company that is importing and exporting goods, or it might be a service company who's providing IT installations or Logistics consultations.

If a consultant proceeds to give you quotation without knowing your purpose, it is not a good consultant but just someone who is rushing to meet his company target and does not really care what are your specific needs.

Perhaps that jurisdiction does not work for you!!

The requirements to open a company in UAE are quite easy and straightforward.

1. Basic Documentation
-This includes a valid passport copy (at least 3 months)
-UAE entry stamp or visa

The second one is basically the stamp that you get in your passport at immigration. We could bypass this requirement if needed and we can tell you how if you write us on info@plutusfinancialprotection.com

-Business Plan
This has to explain the activity you want to start, mention few suppliers and few competitors and the market you wish to operate.

For most Business to Business (B2B) activities, these are ALL requirements to open a company abroad.

What is **NOT** needed:
-Proof of capital
-Utility Bills*

These types of licenses are limited to conduct activities B2B, this means they are not best indicated to conduct activities where there is a product exchange with the general public (supermarkets, hotels, restaurants etc.) but they are just perfect if the activities are related to services like consulting or intermediary or to relocate your funds in another jurisdiction and obtain a residency out of it as well.

Not everyone is satisfied with the grind of a nine to five job in the corporate world, and many people choose to take their knowledge, skills, and experience with them to another, more lucrative industry: consulting.

A consultant is someone who has a unique set of skills and talents that help to create the value-adding components that their clients' businesses lack. The value that they add comes from two sources: content expertise and process expertise.

Content expertise is earned through study and work in a specialized field, where the wealth of your experience and professional relationships lie. In other words, this is your professional "comfort zone" where you are the most competent.

This expertise is rooted in the specific skills and talents that made you successful in one particular industry or field of study in the first place. If you are consulting for a specialized firm for example, as an expert witness in a legal dispute – then you are acting as a content consultant.

This contrasts with **process expertise**, which transcends specific industries, is applicable in almost any environment and involves a set of highly effective methods.

Process expertise is often more valuable than content consulting. It has a wider range of applications across many industries.

Solo consulting is not just amassing and manage a large fortune. In fact, success in consulting involves a huge learning curve and a collection of broad and diverse experience and skills. It brings the possibility to make changes that can potentially impact the lives of tens of thousands of people.

Some people just open the consulting company for funds relocation or to obtain a second residence.

A consultancy business can be started either with a freezone business setup or an offshore business setup and even a traditional mainland company setup.

The main difference with offshore and free zone business set-up instead is in the anonymity: offshore companies do not show the owner even on the trade license.
Again, I suggest referring to your trusted consultant to know the best structure for your goals.

Non-Freezone (Onshore) business setup

The main difference between an onshore and an offshore/freezone company, in UAE, is the presence of a local partner.

In an onshore, Mainland LLC, the local partner needs to own on paper 51% of the company.

Although, this can be left on paper only and agree on a lump-sum for the local sponsor, I recommend using this type of jurisdiction only if your business is Business To Consumer (B2C).
Example can be yachts rentals, restaurants, pizza places, retail shops etc.

Success Story

Blanca is from Brazil. She has always had the dream of owning her own beauty salon but was always discouraged from the safety of her town.
Blanca decided to move to Dubai, UAE.
She also was motivated to find a prime location in the Dubai Marina, so she went to look for every single shop that was appealing for her, studied the footfall of it and proceeded to some offers.
Eventually Blanca found her preferred spot and managed to negotiate a great price.
She then afterwards setup her LLC local company and started to operate.
Blanca now is opening her 5th Beauty Salon.

Opening your LLC company will require a local sponsor so you can either find him alone which is not recommended, or you can rely on trusted consulting companies to source him.

If you have your business abroad or if the purpose of the company is just the residence, I recommend always a free-zone business setup.

How to setup a freezone or offshore Company

Setting up a freezone or offshore company is easier than you think.

In most jurisdiction, you can even do it remotely, by providing the followings to your trusted consultant:

- Clear colored passport copy (all 4 corners of the passport showing)
- Passport photo (shoulders and head showing, colored, white background, dark clothing, no jewelry, eyewear, no teeth)
- UAE entry stamp/residents visa copy (if available)
- 3 suggested names for the business
- Summary of Company Activity (brief description of what the company is going to do)
- Utility Bill (only for offshore)

Looks easy right? Well it is. Most of the times the full company documents can be obtained within a week.

How and why setup a Holding Company

Opening a Freezone Holding company is not reserved only to big and listed companies who divide their business lines and then they have a mother company who owns the share.

Holding company can be used from any individual who:

- Doesn't want the property of their companies to be "traced"
- Wants his assets (especially real estate) protected as are not under personal property

Holding Companies reduce your risk of exposure

Let's say you own companies. This companies are under personal liability. What happens if things go bad?
Well, you will have to liquidate also your personal assets to pay your debtors.

Having a holding company as owner of your "running" company reduces this risk.

Now, let's say you own several real estate assets and you will go through divorce. The assets will have to be liquidated and divided between parts. Holding company avoids that.

Holding Companies optimize your taxation

Your dividends and profits can be transferred to your holding company without incurring in any taxation.
And if you have a "special" residence or citizenship you can even send your funds to your personal accounts without incurring in any taxation.

Holding Companies reorganize your assets and protect yourself to legal or fiscal implications

Having all your assets organized under the property of several holding companies makes it difficult if not impossible to be traced or liquidated.

Ultimately, having holding company offer the following benefits:

- **Unanimous Ownership of Assets and/or Participation in other companies**
- **Optimize taxation in terms of profits distribution**
- **Reorganize your assets ownership and helps you in investment and real estate planning.**

It is extremely easy nowadays to open a Holding Company.
The first step is to choose the jurisdiction which we can consider to be UAE in this case.

I usually recommend an Offshore in case you own several real estate assets or a Free zone in all other cases.

Holding company will not offer you the benefit of having a residence and this is important to keep in mind as if maintaining let's say, an European Passport with European Residence you will still incur into taxation on your personal income so it's important to keep the funds in your holding company and use them from there or move them only when your personal status is "DeTaxed".

You can open the company with just a passport copy and a UAE entry stamp, together with a filled application form and even remotely, without visiting the country.

Again, this is a procedure but for specific cases I always recommend you book a consultation with a trusted consultant. As a reader of this book you are entitled to book a FREE consultation with Plutus Financial Protection.

You just need to send your details to info@plutusfinancialprotection.com mentioning DETAX2320 in the subject, and one of our qualified consultants will get in touch with you.

What I did with holding company

On a personal level, I opened a holding company when I was already owner of 2 companies and several stock market investments.

I reconciled all my investments into the holding company as I did not want to be liable in any way personal and to protect all my investments and assets from any legal implication that might occur in future. Having my own holding company permitted me also to better plan my investments, as knowing that every action is better protected made me make better decisions as well.

All my dividends and profits come to a single place now, it is easier to control, it is more productive, and it is more protected.

Opening a holding company costs less than what you think so I really believe anyone who owns either real estate or paper or business participations in terms on assets should look at this structure as a great opportunity.

How to Open a Corporate Bank Account

So, let's say you opened already your company in United Arab Emirates.

You got your residence, you got your "detaxed" personal status but now you want to start your business and you want to start to generate financial resources.

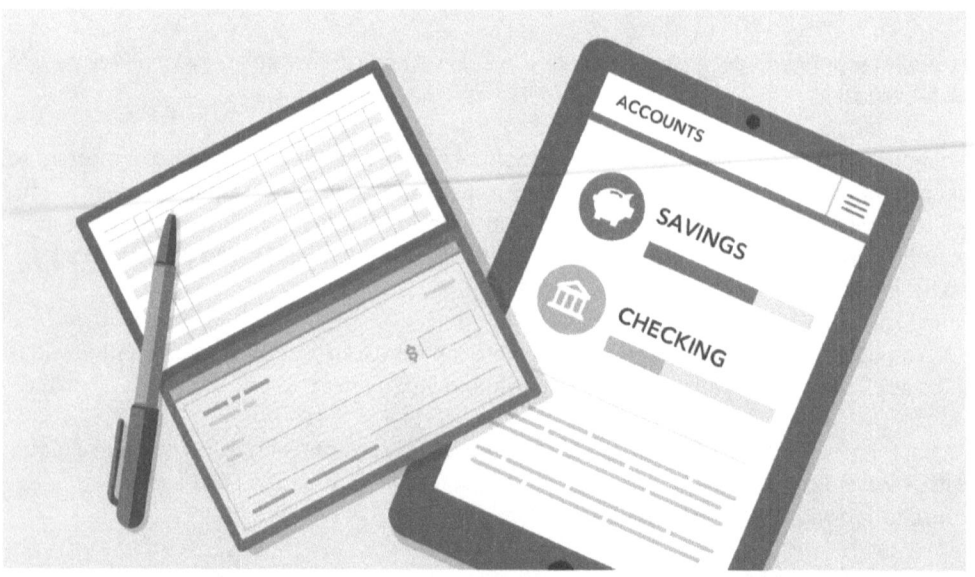

You need to receive payments, which is the main thing.

To receive payments apart from the traditional cash basis you will need to accept payments through wire transfers or credit card payments.

You don't want to invoice your customers with a personal bank account as it does not look professional and perhaps, they cannot even pay you on personal account because of their own company policies.

Also, your customers won't be able to process any credit or debit card payment versus a personal bank account.

You need a company bank account.

To open any company bank account in UAE, you will need the following requirements:

- Company License (free zone, onshore, offshore)
- Passport copy
- Residence Visa (UAE)
- Emirates ID

There is a way to open a company bank account without UAE residence, and you might get to know how if you book a consultation with Plutus or if you get in touch with any other qualified consultant, but for now we will talk about opening a standard bank account.

There are several banks in UAE, all of them having online banking, international services and several branches. The difference between them varies in terms of fees, minimum balances etc.
A google research might inform you about more, common banks are:

- Emirates NBD
- Emirates Islamic Bank
- RAKBANK
- Noor Bank
- Mashreq

Many customers have a lot of difficulty opening a company account even if they have all the requisites above.

How can you successfully open your bank account?

By following the 3 tips that I will expose here.

1. Have a Valid Business Plan.

Bank account opening starts with your professional banker, but it has to go through a compliance process.

Compliance needs to follow anti-money-laundering policies, so they are always questioning the source of the funds you intend to put initially in your account, and they are questioning the real nature of your business.

To overcome this difficulty, you can prepare a 6-7 pages business plan explaining your activity. It does not need to be too much detailed, just make sure you explain the following:

- Nature of your business and your main business lines (example: trading in shoes, furniture and home appliances)
- List your main suppliers
- Explain your target market and the main customers you will be targeting
- Hiring expectancy for the first year
- 1-year financial projections

Sometimes they might ask about the existence of your website, to add more credibility to your company. If you have it prepared that's good, otherwise your consultant might also refer you to low-costs website developers.

2. Have a CV supporting the activity you are starting.

What happens after compliance examines your business plan? they will start questioning the ability of the owner to execute his business plan.

If you are starting a consulting activity, make sure your CV shows experience in consulting. Same thing if you are starting a trading activity.

Keep in mind that the CV is just a word or pdf document and you can make it yourself, they will not do a background check on you as you are not applying for a job!

3. Have valid financials to initially fund your business.

Many bankers will hate me for this free advice I'm giving you, but it is what it is.
The professional banker that is opening the bank account for you has to go through a lot of work and a lot of admin work.
If he knows that you intend to fund your account with 3 or 4 thousand Euro, he will find any possible excuse to tell you that is not possible to open your bank account as he will want to focus on bigger clients.

The key here is to at least communicate them your intention to fund your account with at least 20,000 Euro. This way be sure the process will move much smoother.

Then it is up to your professionality if you intend to keep your word or not.

The Freelance Permit

Freelancing has become increasingly popular in the United Arab Emirates, and thankfully Freelance Permits are now available in many Free Zones based in Dubai, Ras Al Khaimah and Abu Dhabi.

These permits allow for specialized individuals in the media, technology and education sectors to offer their services on a consultancy basis, even if they have a full time job – this initiative has become legalized (with the correct permit) by the United Arab Emirates to boost diverse skills into the local market.

Now you have the opportunity of enjoying tax-free income coming from the S quadrant.

Freelancer Permits can be obtained from Twofour54, Dubai Media City (DMC), Dubai Knowledge Park (DKP), Dubai Internet City (DIC), Dubai Development Authority (DDA) and Ras Al Khaimah Economic Free Zone Authority (RAKEZ).

Currently, individuals based in the following sectors can apply for a permit, these include:

- Media: Actors, journalists, film directors, editors, photographers, writers, animators, artist, audio/sound engineer, brand consultant, cameraman, choreographers, commentators, composers, content provider, copywriters, creative directors, critics, events planners, designers, journalists, lighting specialists, market analysts, marketing specialists, musicians, PR specialists, print media specialists, social media specialists, social media influencers, translators, stylists, web developers/designers plus other more specified roles within the above-mentioned specialties.

- Technology: Web/mobile/software development and architecture, IT and telecommunication networking, data science and analytics, customer service

- Education: Educational advisor, eLearning advisor, executive coach, researcher, trainer

Freelancing is also a way to start your investment career by starting to capitalize on your current skills, open a personal bank account and getting a UAE residence.

Once you get your own residence in UAE, and you register also in the consulate of your own country, you are DeTaxing your own status.

This means that you are not taxed anymore on your personal and professional income and you can even repatriate the funds produced in UAE without incurring in any taxation.

While the residence process is the same across all nationalities, the consulate subscription might differ, so for specific cases it is always suggested to refer to your trusted consultant.

Now I would like to show in one single story, how a set of values and beliefs lead someone to become successful using this structure such as the Freelance Permit.

Success Story: Walter

Walter Scalzone, at the age of 24 wanted to be financially independent from his family.

His first objective was to become financially free and to satisfy first his most basic needs. He noticed that paying taxes would delay greatly his pursue of financial independence, so he started to explore alternatives.

Walter had a particular ranking regarding his values.

1st Love -wanted to be financially free to create his own family. This is connecting with the second need he was pursuing, which was love.

2nd Career & success – he always wanted to be recognized as a reference in his own industry and as an example.

3rd Money – He realized he could not do things he wanted to because did not have money and he wanted more money so he could concede some holidays or luxuries to his own family.

His personality is a campaigner, which is someone extrovert opened to new experience and adventure who's not afraid to change and move out from his own comfort zone.

The value of "health" scored right after money as he need always to be in shape to excel in his career.

He started his career in UAE, Dubai as an employee and enjoying tax-free income but soon he grow tired of the employee lifestyle.

Walter scored high in freedom, so constantly reporting to an overdemanding management was taking its toll on his psychological health.

Walter always had a passion, a passion to play drums.
He loved playing this instrument as it is a tool to infuse energies in people and also it is also a tool to give back to society, through his own foundation.

One of his goals, infact, was not only to produce tax-free income with an independent job but also to support society, especially children in Africa.

For him, the transition from Employee to Self Employed was scary.

He had to give up a safe and stable income to an unsafe one to follow his passion.

Walter started to be a Musician Freelancer at the same time that he was keeping his Employee job.
But this shortly became not sustainable. As he grew more popular, the number of gigs increased, and he found himself going to his 9-5 job without sleep and without energies.

So he had to prioritize and choose what to pursue.

He relied on himself and started to push himself hard and with self-discipline and confidence.
Walter created his own marketing campaign and managed his own social media.

Especially at the beginning he had this fear of insecurity, but then he gained more confidence securing different performance contracts.

Having this fear pushed himself to do more and to work more.

It was also physically not possible to continue to do both activities at the same time. There was no enough time to do both things.

Walter continued to be an Employee and a Self-Employed Freelancer Musician for over 3 years.

Passion and love lead him to continue his musician work. He could have not forgiven himself to live as employee.

He is not feeling the stress of the work when performing this type of work.

Work became part of his lifestyle. He does not feel the distinction of duty time and free time. He understood all the time is free and the allocation is up to you.

Why he chose the Freelance permit?

In his opinion, this was most convenient and value for money structure and was accepted from his contractors. It was a cost-effective solution and entirely tax free. He allowed him to work anywhere in the world

Walter is also working towards diversification and to make his profession a small business by creating an academy.
He plans to hire and teach new people to perform his profession so transiting from S to B quadrant

---

What is the difference between a Freelancer Permit and a Standard Company?

- Freelancer setup is best indicated for specific art and education professions
- Freelancers cannot hire people
- Freelancers cannot open a company bank account but only a personal one
- The residence visa for freelancer lasts 2 years (renewable) compared to 3
- Freelancers can work both B2B and B2C

CHAPTER SUMMARY

SECRET 1:
You can start your business by keeping your Employee job

SECRET 2:
Opening a consultancy company might get you the residence and the related company bank account. You can then enjoy tax free income or relocate your funds in another jurisdiction

SECRET 3:
Having a holding company protects your assets and your wealth, simple as that

SECRET 4:
Opening a company bank account might be challenging but there are tips and tricks to overcome this difficulty even if your business is brand new

SECRET 5:
The freelance permit also gives you a DeTaxed personal status and allows you to work anywhere in the world marketing your own skills in Media and Education field

CHAPTER 7
Alternative Investments

I decided to dedicate a chapter to Alternative Investments as I consider them not only profitable but also fun.

What happens to couch potatoes? Sitting around all day doing nothing, they get fat. Curiously, the opposite is true with money. Leave it sitting around, and you will find that the total just gets smaller and smaller. You need to send your money to exercise.

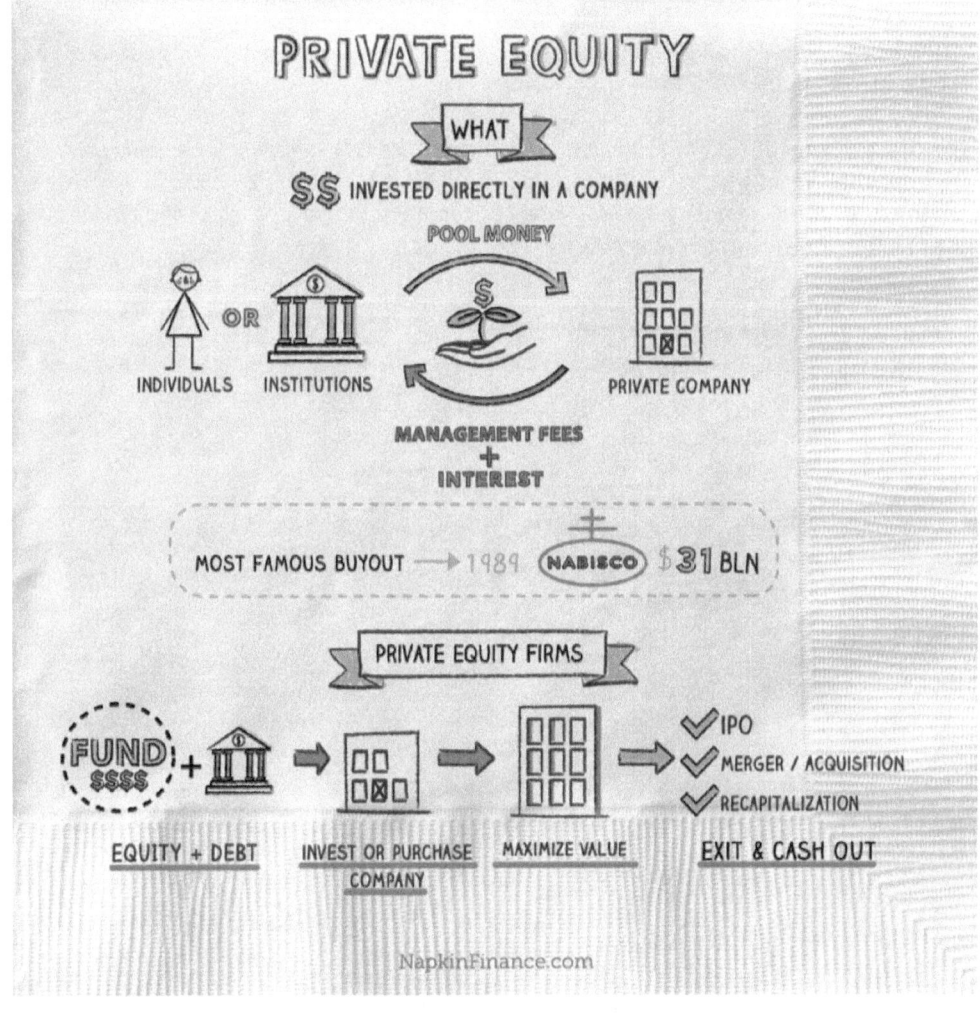

Personal Story in Private Equity

I started my yacht business after my 24th Birthday and since then it has been a pleasure working in Neptune Yachts.

I always wanted to start a business, but I never knew what to start. So I thought: what if I can start something "Fun"?

Having fun while working has been a good prerequisite for growing my own company. Joining alternative investments also might bring a very nice component of fun in your investment career.

Since the beginning, I always joined at least a couple of my own customers trips per week, by giving a "personal touch".

I soon discovered that customization and customer service was something not really taken care from other yacht charter companies, and I decided to make it my own USP.
The structure for this company is a Mainland LLC company with local partner and obviously is not subject to taxation as based in UAE.

What is an "Alternative Investment"?

Alternative Investments is considered pretty much any investment related to Venture Capital and Private Equity.

Every stat-up company needs cash infusion to get started.
Remember the equation of successful business?

Knowledge + Money + Network = Success

You need to have knowledge to start pretty much anything, and with a supporting network you can also reach the third component: money.

You might even start looking for Angel Investors to finance your early startup or you can become an Angel Investor yourself if you have capital.

The term Angel Investor started in Los Angeles in 1920. At that time, wealthy individuals financed first Hollywood films. The term angel later spread to other business fields, and wealthy donors willing to part with cash to benefit young companies were dubbed business angels.

How hard is your money working for you? What are your savings doing right now? If you are like most people, your money probably is staying in your bank account and being hit from inflation.

"Take the leap! Quit your day job and be your own boss!"
Following this type of entrepreneurial advice comes with many risks. We already talked about how smart can be to develop your business as a side business; but how about investing in someone else business, where you do not have to put your own time but only your financial resources?

And let's face it: not everyone who tries self-employment thrives as their own boss. Becoming a company manager means deal with people, finances, payments, marketing, sales, operations…. Doing this requires time, and now perhaps you want to let your money work for you, not yourself work for you.

A side business provides a form of job freedom that absolutely anyone can attain. Even better if you can combine a Side business with some side investments. Remember, it is better to have 10 different sources of incomes of EUR 1,000 then one single source of income of EUR 10,000.

You can even think of it as a kind of job security. The days of a "job for life" are over, nowadays it is crucial to be involved in several fields to diversify and to ensure our future financial needs are covered.

You cannot rely on your employee job to provide alone of all the financial resources that you need or might need in future. What do you think happens if you get terminated from the company you work for?

Everybody needs different sources of income. It can make transitioning from your day job easier, too, if you decide to quit or are fired. Being an alternative investor gives you also tastes of entrepreneurship, with very small risks related involved.

Traditional or Non-Traditional Investing?

Traditional savings methods are not alone effective anymore, that is why I always propose to invest in something alternative. After all, if everyone is investing in the same thing, there would be no profitability in it.
You see those crowd-funding campaign for a new startup? That's an alternative investment.

Alternative investment is considered also an existing local company or SME that is not listed in any stock market but that is offering its shares.

Going in this kind of investment apart from being fun might give you interesting opportunities to grow in a fast-pace industry.

Remember, if this SMEs have been profitable for 5 years consecutive, great chances are that will be profitable in future as well and your investment might even help you grow their business.

I personally recommend investing in a trending industry in that specific market.

You can always send an email to info@plutusfinancialprotection.com to get more information about AI in those incredible existing businesses that might bring fun in your life a part from injecting new financial resources in your wealth.

Alternative investments are usually completely tax-free especially if located in a fiscal jurisdiction where there is no taxation at all.

Also, Alternative Investments rarely have any correlation with any investment you might be involved in, making it an excellent strategy for diversification and to reduce the risk of your overall investment portfolio.

What differentiates alternative investments from traditional investments?

Traditional Investments

Strategies constructed primarily utilizing public stocks and bonds. Characterized by:
- High liquidity profile
- Assets in public markets
- High correlation to markets
- Passive shareholders
- Returns primarily driven by beta with lower dispersion among investors

Alternative Investments

Investments that look to exploit inefficiencies in markets by focusing on non-traditional assets and investment strategies. Characterized by:
- Potential illiquidity
- Assets in private and public markets
- Low correlation to markets
- Active shareholders (at times solo owners)
- Returns primarily driven by alpha with higher dispersion among managers
- Often focused on inefficient markets

With an Alternative Investment, you have also the opportunity of becoming a small business owner, act like one, and make even a difference in the company you invested in.
And the risk is greatly reduced when you can influence yourself the results of a specific company.

"Alternative investors have the power also to influence business decisions, and perhaps make even a great positive influence. This means that they get more control over their investment than they would get by investing in traditional stocks. "

Given the low liquidity of these types of investment, is always recommended to consult your trusted financial advisor as you might need to be able to cope to long time before you are going to sell this type of investment but depending on the conditions you can enjoy very high dividends and perhaps get your full investment back even in only 3 or 4 years.

Some Hedge Funds active in this field ask at least 500,000 EUR to be able to enter but through Plutus Financial Protection LLC you might be able to find options that are as low as 20,000 EUR.

Cryptocurrency is considered also an alternative investment as well and you might consider starting to study about it as it is and will change the way we perceive money.

Ultimately, alternative investments can offer investors a much-needed source of higher returns and risk diversification that are simply non-existent in the world of traditional investing.

Many people think, "I could never start my own business.". Starting a business only requires a bit of creativity but even if you don't want to go through that path, there are many alternative investment options in private equity that you can join with minimal capital exposure and sometimes benefit from the booming of them.

Michael Dell started Dell computers by working part-time in his university dorm room and eventually got so rich that he decided to drop out. Well, you can join many private equities emerging before the boom.

Some facts

In the investment's world, methods and techniques are useful but not infallible.

Once again, I would like to stress on the important of diversification. Even the investments taken from my team in the recreation business, are subject to tourism trends, seasonal weather, overall economy. Diversification plays a major role to protect your wealth.

Investing is a fun game. By studying the investment world, you can benefit from knowing another people's mistake before making your own.
If you are a starter, and had some successful moves, do not fall in the trap of overconfidence: it can backfire quickly.
Emotions like fear, anger, envy and greed are your investment portfolio's worst nightmare.
Before starting any investment, do your due diligence or ask help to professionals.

What to invest in?

Through these chapters we examined different ways to protect your wealth, to setup your company, to adapt the right financial management habits and to know about private equity and alternative investment.

Now maybe you want to know about different ways to make money

Well, let's start with a bit of autobiography.

The goal of this book is to create the financial resources and protect them, in order to support your dream lifestyle.

This was my goal as well.

At the age of 19 I set a goal: in 10 years' time I did not want to need to work for money. I took 11 years to achieve this goal but eventually I made it.

Being billionaire was not my goal, I was never interested in luxury and show-off, but I wanted to reach a status where I was free to work, free to play, free to travel.

Now, if this is your goal as well, you might want to examine different ways of investing like I did.

Stock market

I have invested heavily in the stock market, particularly in stocks and options and at this stage the income deriving from them supports alone my lifestyle.

It is not an easy path, but I believe everyone should have income deriving from it. You will not become Warren Buffet and after reading many books on him I realized that traditional investment techniques will not make you reach that status.

Warren Buffet, for example, made 600 M USD net profit on a deal on Goldman Sachs he was able to get only when the company was in a very bad state and investing 6B USD getting privileged stocks. Privileged stocks mean that in case of bankruptcy of the company, his stocks would be the first ones to be reimbursed. This means that the risk of losing this money was very very low.
This kind of investments is inaccessible to the most of us that is why I don't recommend to set a goal of income deriving from the stock market that is that high but Instead I would aim to get a humble 1,000/2,000 EUR per month from investments that can already support alone a decent lifestyle.

Before investing in the stock market, you might want to get a company in UAE first and a related residence.
Why? To get a non-taxation status. Traditionally, a European citizen and resident pays 27.5% taxes on capital gain.

This means that you are taking 100% the risk and 72.5% of the gain while the government is getting 27.5% without taking any risk. This sentence is self-explanatory right?

Regarding the products you might look at, I use a value investment – low stress – approach.

Be updated about what is happening around you. Read the news and have an idea about trending industries. Afterwards, go analyzing the companies with low Price/Earnings and high dividend yield in that industry. A <20 P/E and a dividend yield >3% is already a good indicator.

A positive Return on Investment (ROI) and Return on Equity (ROE) and a low debt are other great indicators to tell you to invest in that specific company.

You might want to protect your investment, and buy an option put on the same stock with expiry 3 months later and strike price at the money. This strategy is called "Protective Put".

These are the types of investments I do 80% of the times and that bring me steady income and low losses given the diversification.

A good diversification is enough with six different types of stocks, you do not need to buy the full exchange like many people believe.

I understand these are very technical terms, so I suggest another research on option strategies or book a consultation with Plutus to go more in detail.

Real Estate

Real Estate is a great source of income, especially if you have possibility to get mortgage at low rates.

Buying an apartment paying 3% per year of interest rate, and then renting it out for a 7% return per year brings you a return of 4% and the best part out of it is that you are not using your money but the banks.

Private Equity

Private equity brings higher return and more control on the investment given the personal touch related to it. We spoke already a lot about alternative investments, you might have a look at them on many crowd funding platforms or enquiring at info@plutusfinancialprotection.com

There are many other ways in making money, I personally tried network marketing; affiliate marketing with shopify; and different other ways too but in my experience, they have not been worth the time spent into it so I won't suggest them.

Paper Assets & Alternative Investments, with an optimized taxation status setup have been the most successful in my experience.

CHAPTER SUMMARY

SECRET 1:
Start investing! Make your money work for you. Investing in private equity might be very profitable and rewarding

SECRET 2:
Multiple streams of income are extremely important. Secure first your Zero tax status, then you might want to start investing in stock market as well

SECRET 3:
Being an alternative investor will give you also the knowledge and the connections to potentially start your own business in the future

CHAPTER 8
The essentials of running a business

This chapter is a bonus as at this point, I assume you already have knowledge of your psychology, adopted tricks to improve your physical shape and created an optimized taxation status for yourself and for your company.

In this status I want to talk about some essentials of running a business since it has been proposed several times to create a company abroad... so why not start to make it profitable as well?

Now you need few things for starting your business.
Did you know that Bill Gates did not invent the software that made him the world's richest man? He merely bought it from a group of programmers. He built a great business, not a great product – and that was the key to his success.

Building a business is a matter of mastering three things.

First, a business needs a spiritual mission to guide it.

Finding a guiding spiritual mission, one that aligns with your financial goals, will help keep you on the right track.

Second, every leader needs a team.

Maybe you are an accountant, a salesman or a lawyer but it is unlikely that you are all three and all are important if you want a successful business. You team is your investment. Examine yourself and hire people that have the skills that you don't have. Or you can hire people that have mastered certain skills you have in a better way.

Third, every team needs a leader

Leadership is not about being the best, is about bringing the best in people.
Individuate the skills and the strength in your team and leverage them. Encourage people not to fix their weaknesses but to leverage their strengths.

Now, let's assume you opened already your company. You got your residence visa and you opened your bank account.

Company Identity

Starts by defining a vision and a mission for your company.

Vision is the ultimate goal for your company
Mission is how the company plans to achieve this mission

Example, for Plutus Financial Protection LLC:

Vision: Become the advisor that help people protecting their wealth and focusing on what they love
Mission: Through the creation of ad-hoc companies that minimize taxation and proposal of alternative investment solutions that develop investments portfolios.

For the other company, Neptune Yachts Rental LLC:

Vision: Being the yacht charter venue that creates unforgettable emotions for its customers

Mission: To provide affordable customized yacht charter solutions according to the occasion

Define a mission that transforms people's lives and tell it with a gripping story.

Letting customers know that your company works for great things is vital, and the tool to get you there is a powerful mission that is well communicated. Here's how to make it happen:

First of all, your mission should involve presenting something that transforms your customers' lives. To that end, it's essential that companies work hard to produce innovative ideas that can truly make a difference. And do not underestimate the emotional touch: remember this, **people will forget who you are but will not forget how you made them feel**.

Some examples.
Google set out to make all the information in the world organized and accessible. Their path to doing so was a conspicuous reinvention of the concept of a search engine from 1998 onwards. In the process, they earned themselves a spot in the dictionary, becoming synonymous with the act of researching something over the internet.

Google radically transformed the way people find information and ultimately improved the lives of consumers.

But having a mission alone is not enough, it is also important to build a compelling narrative around it. For that, you need a brand story composed of three elements: character, plot and metaphor.

First, a brand becomes a character when it represents something good valued by society. An example would be Disney, which represents family ideals. It is not about your values anymore now; it is about your customers' values.

Then, to make that character relevant to the lives of customers, it's necessary to have a captivating plot. One strategy is to use a challenge plot, a story in which your brand battles a stronger opponent and wins.

For example, The Body Shop tells the story of farmers in developing countries who are engaged in the struggle for fair trade.

You will need online resources too, as people nowadays spend most of their times online and not offline.

A **website**. This is your online home, and a content-management system such as WordPress can make setting it up easy. Or you can refer to marketing agencies to build your website if you do not have the expertise to dedicate to it by yourself

A **social media profile** is also equally important.
You don't need to operate on every single platform – just one or two should be fine. However, do register your business name with the most popular platforms, such as Facebook or Twitter, irrespective of your current reach.

Setup a **payment system**. Be sure to have an invoicing system, PayPal account or shopping cart on your website before you launch.

Once you have these elements sorted out, you should prioritize providing more value and generating more money. Value is best improved by responding to customers' unspoken needs.

When you're selling a product or service, you've really got to emphasize its merits. Lead with the benefits. You might tell customers that your product or service will make them happier or their lives simpler and better.

Ideally, you should connect with people's emotions.

Consider a dog sitter. She might not explicitly try to assuage an owner's guilt about leaving his dog at home alone, but she can imply it. Emotions sell.
A carefully crafted pitch might go "Leave your dog with me and he'll feel loved and cared for." Be subtle.
Once you're able to distill your business benefits, you should reach out to four types of people who can help you along the way. There's no need to do your solo side project alone.

Keith Ferrazzi in his book "Never Eat Alone" goes in details about how to find and leverage connectors and super connectors.

First, find **supporters**. Most likely this means your family and friends – people who can contribute in different ways and support your efforts.
Second, seek out **mentors**. These are guides or experts who can give you feedback and advice. Third, identify **influencers**. These are trendsetters who'll spread the news about your product. Trusted authorities, like reviewers or bloggers, are generally best for this. Fourth, locate some **ideal customers**.

These people are perfectly placed to evaluate products and respond to questions you might have with honest and detailed answers.

Once you've established this network, you're sure to go far. And make sure you find agents, i.e. people that can refer business to you as soon as possible. Agents can be considered anyone who refers your business in exchange of commission. Don't be stingy on commissions: remember that you wouldn't have reached this kind of customer if it wasn't for the agent.

Often, when business owners are asked how their businesses are going, they'll just respond "yes all good". This is not a right answer. A business is going either upwards or downwards. Make sure your business is always in an upward trend, even if slight.

It's important, in the early stages of your business, to know exactly what sort of trajectory your business is on.
Once you're up and running, ask yourself a simple question: is your venture making money? There are three possible answers.

First, you might find you're far exceeding initial expectations. Fine, that's great. You've obviously got to keep going.

Second, you might think your original idea was good, but people haven't latched onto it. It's difficult to admit it, but that's the time to cut your losses and move on. This happened to myself in one of my first ventures: the pizza place in the UAE that I had to close and move on after only two months.

The most common response in the early stages is the third. You've found your idea hasn't completely gained traction, but as it's making a bit of money it doesn't make sense to pull the plug.
If this last option sounds familiar, but you're still not certain how to finesse the problem areas in your business, then have a look at your metrics.

Metrics are measured in three areas. Profit – that's income minus expenses. Growth – ask yourself how many new customers or what new prospects you have. And time – how long do you spend on your new side business each week? If the time you spend in your business is increasing, it is not a good sign. Remember that you want your business to grow and your involvement in it to decrease. This might mean working 18h a day at the beginning but ultimately you want to dedicate to it less than 10 hours per week.

Once you've identified areas of concern, you can improve on them by applying two basic rules. In the first case, do more of what's working. In the second, abandon what's not. It's universally tempting to try to solve a problem. But don't. Really. The most successful people just drop them and concentrate more on those aspects that function best. You do not have to solve everything. You can also choose to disappear and let your staff handle problems, you will be surprised to notice how many issues are solved without your intervention.

Lead Generation

Having clients, I consider the most important step of making your company profitable. Especially at the beginning, you will need the cashflow from these clients to invest in marketing.

You can generate Leads through different channels

- Online: through your website, social media and paid ads.
- Offline: by being member of well-established networking organizations and joining regularly exhibitions, networking events, etc.
- Partnership with referral partners: why not relying of "external sales teams"? try to individuate fast who are the referral partners and be generous with the commissions, they will be worth.

In my failed pizza place, I missed this point miserably. I was counting on the pizza place to be supported from the orders generated from the yacht, but I soon realized that a restaurant fixed costs are too high; therefore I should have planned to generate leads from as many channels as possible and not relying on one only.

Marketing 101 and the 4 P.

The 4 P. of marketing are following:

Product: your product or service must be as much as possible differentiated from competitors and provide a value-added solution to your clients or solve their problems.

Price: your price should be fair and justify its value, especially when compared to competitors.

Place: your product or service must be offered from the right channels to be profitable

Promotion: your product or service need to have a valid promotion to appear attractive to your customers

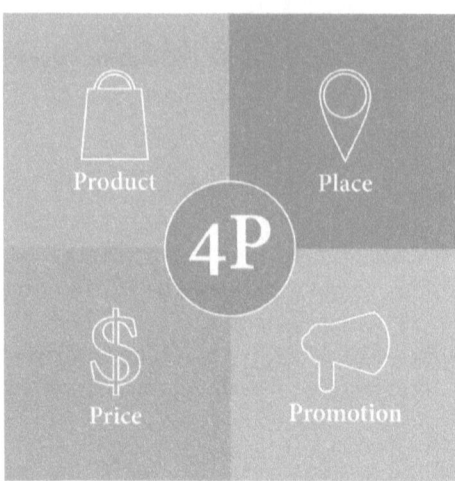

For your product or service, you need to define an USP which is "Unique Selling Point" Basically, your USP should determine your competitive advantage and most of all should determine your Value Proposition.

Value Proposition can be added features, added possibilities to upgrades or in case of service might be superior customer service or emotions.

Focus on the biggest customer pains or problems for your value propositions. For functional jobs, ask questions like, "How can I save customers time and money?" (One option might be to offer discounted installation services.) For social jobs, ask, "Can I help customers be seen favorably by others?" Perhaps you can offer an online social platform where people share photos of their flourishing gardens.

Then, you need to make your product or service appealing. Remember that image is extremely important that is why many food companies invest into nice packaging.

After defining your product or service, you need to make it accessible.
Location might be extremely important in food businesses or any business that depends on foot fall. Having your business in an accessible spot, which is also very high in foot fall is certainly a recipe for success.

After determining the place where your product or service is located, you need to put a price to it.
Pricing might be tricky as it has to take in consideration how much customers in that area are willing to spend and also how much your competitors are pricing similar product/service. In my yacht business, I focused on a very simple competitive strategy: "lower price and higher quality than my competitors"

Now that you've designed the initial value proposition for your product or service, the location and the price, you can define a specific promotion to make it shine in front of your customer's eyes.

The goal is for your value proposition to lead you to a profitable business. Generally speaking, this happens when the revenue you generate exceeds the costs of your business. Whether you're trying to sell a sprinkler system or a fashionable pair of shoes, you'll only succeed if your value proposition generates more revenue than costs.

Don't be the next Ford Edsel

Have you ever heard of the Ford Edsel? Originally intended to be Ford's flagship product in the late 1950s, the car not only ended up being one of the most spectacular product failures of all time but is also frequently cited as one of the ugliest cars ever made.

How could a company as successful as Ford fail?
For one, it completely miscalculated the market.

In 1955, the American automobile market was booming. Families' disposable income was increasing, and people were becoming more interested in medium-priced cars, a segment in which Ford was weak.
That's when the company started planning the Ford Edsel.

Unfortunately, by the time the Edsel was launched in 1958, the market had done a 180: an economic downturn and an abrupt change in consumer tastes had made people stick to smaller and cheaper car models.

A second reason for the failure was that customers had unrealistic expectations for the car. Ford had spent $250 million on planning the Edsel, making it the company's most expensive project up to that point – a fact that Ford promoted extensively in its marketing. This created a lot of buzz around the project, so when the Edsel was finally launched, consumers were expecting something revolutionary.
However, they were disappointed to see that the Edsel was just another four-wheeled automobile after all.

The third and final strike for the Edsel was its shoddy build. Since Ford had spent most of its efforts on carrying out psychological research to make the car appealing to its target group (i.e., young families with a disposable income), it neglected to fine-tune the technical side of the car. Consequently, once the product launched, customers found several faults, ranging from unreliable brakes to a jumpy acceleration.
Although the Edsel might not have been a completely useless car in the end, it just couldn't live up to its expectations.

The VCP Model

The VCP Model stands for:

- Visibility
- Credibility
- Profitability

Ultimately, to get the profitability for your business and to develop it, you need to be as much as possible visible

This means that you can use a combination of all your marketing tools that need to be adapted to your product and service.

You wonder why you have never seen a Lamborghini ad in television?
Well, because it is expansive to reach a very large client base and then possibly very few of people that watch TV are a target client for Lamborghini.

Plan smartly and invest your funds in marketing wisely.
Networking events are again recommended as they have the chance to make the management directly visible.

You should also be credible to your clients because ultimately people buy from people who they trust.

Referrals also are extremely important in UAE as they generate almost 70% of every business income.

Referrals are recommendations for your company made by customers or partners to new prospective customers. They are essential to any in-depth marketing strategy and can make all the difference between a floundering start-up and the next big thing.

To make your company "referral worthy" six aspects are essential. Combined, they make up what is known as a referral engine, a machine that will prospect your company to success.

Humans usually share information they trust, and this can be used at your own advantage.

The social nature of humanity means people want to make referrals as a means of earning recognition. This makes perfect sense when you consider that, within tribal societies, maintaining good social standing was a precondition for survival. After all, failing to make people like and value you could mean rejection from the tribe and probably death as well.

As a result, a deep desire for social validation is hardwired into our brains. In fact, the quest for validation from others is so deep within us that it's controlled by the same part of the brain that is responsible for primitive functions like eat, drink and sleep.

To benefit from this impulse to earn social validation, your business should only present relevant and useful information. For example, telling another tribe member about a good hunting spot in a time of famine would naturally earn the referrer a good deal of respect.

To make matters more complicated, building trust is a long-term game, requiring commitment and consistency.
Why a customer refers you? It is an essential question that your strategy must address.
You have to offer something different that people will talk about or identify a way that you already do.
To do this, you need to innovate by doing things differently in a proven market or simplifying the product you already offer.

Businesses with a social mission, like TOMS shoes, offer an inspiring example. TOMS donate a pair of shoes to a needy child for every pair that it sells, in the process differentiating itself in an authentic way and leading it to great success.

Also, sometimes getting more customers is not always a good thing. Having the right kind of customers will increase the positive experiences your clients have, thereby producing buzz for your business.
Remember that the customer is not always right, and sometimes is more positive to decline troublesome customers instead of taking them onboard.

Sometimes when I see difficult customers, with very high and unrealistic expectations, I prefer to decline them instead of dealing with them with troublesome complains or negative reviews. Think it like the missed revenue as a marketing investment.

Not all customers are a match for your business, but you can identify which ones are by creating a profile of your ideal one. Just think of a current customer who brings you the most profit, loyalty and referrals.

From there, be as detailed as possible: incorporate real customer stories, ask questions about the challenges your customers face, the people they trust and, finally go to the customers who already refer your business to ask them why they do so.

For instance, the customer profile for a home renovation company might be married homeowners with a combined income of over 100,000 EUR, who are entrepreneurial and have a long-term plan for their lives. They are engaged in their local community, have no intention of moving and have renovated before.

Then, with your customer profile in hand, you can produce a key story that will engage your customers emotionally. This is essentially a narrative that you convey through your actions, marketing and branding.

Build strategic partnerships

Strategic partners are businesses with a common ideal customer and reaching out to them is vital.

You can start by listing the high-quality companies you trust and would happily recommend to your own referral stars.
It's good to start with businesses you personally know and use.
From there, send a letter of introduction to each of them, communicating that you have customers who might be interested and that you'd like to learn more about the company.

For instance, you could request information about their value proposition and post-referral marketing procedure.

After identifying potential partners who are interested, your job is to help them recognize partnership opportunities in which you both gain something.

Remember that you need to start by helping them, try to understand their business first and try to generate referral for them in first instance, afterwards they will for sure send referrals back to you as recognition, even if this recognition might come in a later stage it is always worth to follow this method.

Joint marketing ventures can be an extremely productive use of your partnerships. For instance, in a three-way partnership between an electrical contractor, a plumber and a heating and cooling business, all three parties could hand out one another's marketing materials and coupons.

One of the best things about partnerships is that those with a certain edge of creativity to them are especially buzzworthy. Just take one IT company that offered free massages during its recruitment presentation. This odd stunt got the company the attention of the top accountants it was seeking, while earning new clients for the massage therapists involved.

Look at complementary industries also for your business. If your service has add-ons, building strategic partnerships with add-ons providers might be beneficial for the both of you.

Accurate financial management

As you are by now keeping a very nice track of your personal finances, you should do exactly the same with your company finances.

I usually suggest outsourcing entirely your accounting department especially at the beginning as it might not be worth to pay a salary full time to an accountant that maybe you need once a week.

New business models are bypassing the traditional concepts of ownership and middlemen Back in the day, a business could be accurately valued by taking stock of its physical assets. But this doesn't apply to companies like Airbnb and Uber, which have no actual rooms or cars of their own. So how does Airbnb get valued at $30 billion and Uber at $66 billion?

They create a peer-to-peer marketplace by operating software that acts as the middleman between their clients, who own the apartments and cars, and their users, who want to temporarily use this property.

This model is also known as "access-instead-of-ownership" and part of the platform's success is due to its collaborative nature, matching, for example, users seeking lodging with those who already own apartments that they can rent out. In addition, both parties can choose whether or not they want to do business with the other based on ratings from previous transactions.

And innovative blockchain technology promises to take this model to the next level by vaporizing even more middlemen.
Blockchain technology relies on the principles of cryptography to allow for business transactions between two parties without any company or banking oversight, and thus without any associated fees.
It's already being used for Bitcoin, the electronic currency.
Platforms operating on blockchain payments can be completely independent of banks and credit card companies that take big percentages on transactions and sell user data for dubious purposes. A "blockchain" version of Airbnb, for instance, could allow users and owners to save money.

Another example of a streamlined service is crowdfunding, which is making it easier for entrepreneurs to find funding.
Crowdfunding bypasses the slow, traditional process of raising investor funds by getting rid of the paperwork and endless interviews. It puts the power in the hands of individuals to reach out on a software platform, attract investors through incentives and even integrate feedback during the development process.

Protect your Company's Wealth!

Don't be subject to fines for missed licenses or missed reports. By now you should have understood that sometimes protecting what you already have is more important than getting more.

Warren Buffett is one of the richest people on the planet, and yet he admits that his tax rate is lower than his secretary's (whose income, naturally, amounts to far less than his). Sound like a cruel joke?

Well, it's the perfect example of how unfair the US federal income tax system is. To understand how it got so bad, let's examine the increasingly twisted development of the system since its inception.

In 1913, after decades of political debate and fears that it was tantamount to socialism, the federal government began to levy an income tax.
The reason was that its own income stream had run dry while its expenses were increasing.

Initially, income tax rates were low, and the main contributors were the richest citizens. Since then, rates have been raised continually and the application of the tax expanded to larger swathes of the population and, at the same time, more and more loopholes were created for the rich.

These days, the income tax rates are generally quite high and have the greatest effect on the middle-class population.

The way the tax is structured today encourages inefficiency. For example, freelancers will often stop taking on new contracts mid-way through the year just to not earn more income because, from a tax perspective, it makes more sense than earning more.

What's more, the complicated system of loopholes has made enforcing taxation a battle. The Internal Revenue Service, which collects the tax, must annually contend with an army of citizens' tax advisers and lawyers whose specialty is circumventing the tax code.

This is a colossal waste of human resources on both sides. Unfortunately, though, tax reform is politically unfeasible. Multiple presidents have tried to reform the tax code into something simpler, but all have failed. The current system simply favors too many rich people with too much influence, and they don't want to relinquish their advantages, such as capital gains being taxed less than salary income.

So, if you have started your business through Plutus guidance, continue to do so, and manage your DeTaxed financials correctly.

CHAPTER SUMMARY

SECRET 1:
A vision and a mission of your business does not only make you look good in front of potential investors but it is vital to remind owners and managers where to implement the competitive advantage

SECRET 2:
Lead generation might be done in different ways, but before generating high volume leads it is important to have an idea who can be your ideal customer, the one that can also refer you business in future

SECRET 3:
Create a nice financial structure for your business, avoid useless expenses in fines and penalties. Minimize your taxation.

CONCLUSION

Protecting your wealth is extremely important. It is important as much as generating it.

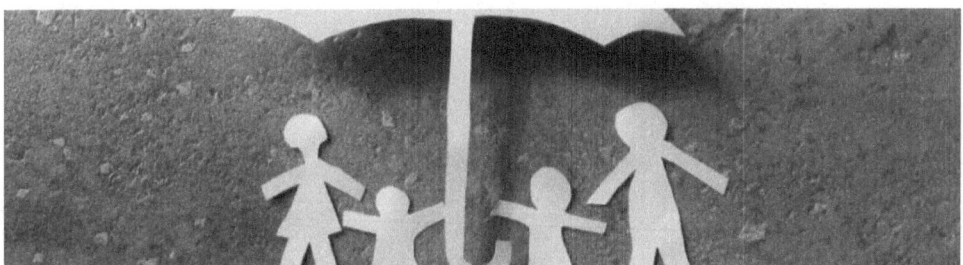

You cannot produce and protect your wealth if you are constantly taxed in the three dimensions of Mind, Body and Finances.

You cannot produce ang protect your wealth if your decisions are not aligned with your values and your personality.
Knowing yourself is a great starting point, because ultimately efficient decisions are the ones synchronized to who we are.
Take a journey to "**go and become**", it might be the best investment of all.
Your needs, your values, your beliefs and your personality are all psychological components that make you the person you are today.

And the metrics used to measure your values are equally important too.

Dave Mustaine, founder of the rockband "Megadeth", although very successful and with all his decisions aligned to his values and personality, condemned himself to a life of unhappiness.
Why? Because he based his success about being more popular and famous compared to the rockband "Metallica".
Not knowing who you are in depth and setting unrealistic goals might bring only unhappiness in your life.
Basing your happiness on external values where you don't have control, also might bring you only unhappiness.

You cannot examine alternative investment opportunities if your body is not fit to travel.
Even if you do not care about your physical appearance that much, remember that:

1. We live in a world where appearance is more important than being

2. Healthy mind lives in a healthy body

If you are not healthy, you will not have the energies to deal with other aspects of your life, plus you do not want to spend time in hospitals, clinics and so on and so forth.

You cannot generate income from different quadrants if you don't optimize your corporate and personal fiscal status. There is a limit how much money you can generate as an employee.
Your time is limited, trading YOUR time for money is not necessarily an efficient idea.
Keep in mind also that avoiding problems is not a solution. Having "good" problems and stresses lead you to a fulfilled and successful life after solving them.

You want to start investing, you want to start generating passive income or you want to protect the income you generated. These are all valid reasons to consider founding a brand-new company in an optimized taxation Nation, such as United Arab Emirates.
Minimizing taxation at the beginning greatly speeds up the process of wealth generation.
And remember to set a clear goal for yourself. Purpose of this book is not how to show you to become a millionaire, but it is to show you how you can setup a **fiscal, financial, body and mind structure to support your dream lifestyle.**

Hopefully by now you found inspiration of new actions, and motivation to pursue your goals.

Remember that the time we have on earth is limited and should not be wasted in a job that you hate because it pays the bills. You should not be limited from financial constraints because you spend half of your life paying taxes.

I hope this book has showed you ways, lessons, and a practical how to not just to "detax" your life but also to improve your overall happiness.

Protect your Wealth, Focus on what you Love